A Winter's Day

A Winter's Day

HENRIK TIKKANEN

Translated from the Swedish by
MARY SANDBACH

PANTHEON BOOKS
NEW YORK

FIRST AMERICAN EDITION

Translation Copyright© 1980
by Mary Sandbach

All rights reserved under International and Pan-
American Copyright Conventions. Published in the
United States by Pantheon Books, a division of Random
House, Inc., New York, and simultaneously in Canada
by Random House of Canada Limited, Toronto. Originally published in Finland as *Brändövägen 8 Brändö Tel. 35*
by Söderströms & Co., Förlags Ab, Stockholm. Copyright ©1976 by Henrik Tikkanen. This translation first
published in Great Britain as *Snob's Island* by Chatto &
Windus, Ltd.

Library of Congress Cataloging in Publication Data

Tikkanen, Henrik.
A winter's day.

Translation of Brändövägen 8, Brändö, Tel. 35.
1. Tikkanen, Henrik—Biography.   2. Authors,
Swedish—20th century—Biography.   I. Title.
PT9876.3.I37Z512513   839.7'3'74   [B]   79-3326
ISBN 0-394-50803-3

Manufactured in the United States of America

THE FIRST PART of a story which teaches that
a man who will not look forward
and cannot look backward
should look out

A Winter's Day

I

This is a gruesome book about sudden death, ruin, adultery, and drink. It tells of the misfortunes of a family and of the struggle against misfortune that is the meaning of life and of its impossibility.

In Finland a story is like a winter's day. Short and dark, and you cannot see anything at a distance. I shall begin my story within my range of vision, but where the story begins I cannot say, nor do I know what it is like. Of course, I shall blame the wrong people. I shall twist and distort everything. I shall wriggle like a worm trying to get off the hook.

Perhaps it is best to blame fate for letting me be born in an impossible country, in which there live a little over three million people whose language is incomprehensible to everyone in the world. And that is not all. In this same country my parents speak another language, which only a tenth of the population understands. Moreover, the way my parents express themselves is such that only a hundredth part of that tenth understands them. In actual fact they don't care a damn for the rest of the people. On the other hand they are magnanimous enough to hate the whole of the Russian people who are their neighbours. Naturally they have never tried to learn Russian, so they don't understand a word of what two hundred million people say or think, and they are proud of it.

In this country I first saw the light of day six years after a victorious war, in which one half of the people

3

had conquered the other half. The victors stopped the mouths of the vanquished who were dumb thereafter for twenty years. Anyone with even the most modest intellectual demands on life would have refrained from being born in this vacuum. But my parents were as irresponsible before my birth as after it. When they had eaten their way through a barbaric Christmas dinner with eleven main courses at my paternal grandmother's, they begot me without a thought of what they were going to do with me. This is best shown by the fact that they engaged a German governess, who taught me German as my first language.

I had three older brothers. None of them spoke German. My father had studied in Dresden and he spoke German, but he had uncommonly little to say to me. My mother spoke quite decent school German, but she was not often at home. My father did not approve of the way in which the governess swallowed the *r* in *Fenster* as the Berliners do. He thought his child spoke with a vulgar accent and, intending to be ironical. he started to call me *Beau* in French.

My brothers, who spoke neither German nor French, changed *Beau* into Bobo, and with this name, best suited to a chimpanzee, I was put to live among people who could only pronounce *b*'s as *p*'s. To them I was Pupu, and in Finnish that means hare. It is not easy being a hare amidst a people who regard themselves as God's chosen heroes.

For it was in Finland that I came to be born. Finland, that was once part of the kingdom of Sweden, then part of the Russian Empire, and at last an independent state which tried to annexe part of Russia, but failed. After this setback a large part of the able-bodied members of the population emigrated to Sweden. Those who were left behind tried to distinguish themselves by being lovers of peace and did their best, under the leadership

4

of a bald President, to build a bridge between East and West.

My father was also bald, and so I had great faith in this President. He was certainly a man of the people. He had been born in a log cabin, though of course he was not to be compared with my father, in spite of the fact that he too began to smoke fat cigars in his old age. He was the seventh President of the country and it was no longer specially grand to be the President. In Finland, you see, only the first is great and can never be surpassed by anyone, however capable he may be. Consequently, Ståhlberg, who was Finland's first President, is the most remarkable of all Presidents; and Finland's first great poet, Runeberg, is greater than all other poets; and Finland's first great runner, Paavo Nurmi, is greater than all other runners; and Finland's first great composer, Sibelius, is greater than all other composers; and Finland's first great Field Marshal, Mannerheim, is greater than all the other generals who ever shot a Bengal tiger. The bald-headed President compensated for not being the first by holding his high office for the longest term. Like Mannerheim he learnt how to handle the Finns from the Russians, and no one dared to remove him or replace him by some-one else as long as it amused him to be President. The result was that under him the country prospered beyond its wildest dreams, which was too heavy a burden for many people to bear. Even the best families provided recruits for the scores of homeless alcoholics and radical revolu-tionaries. And as no external enemy threatened us we had to look for one nearer at hand, and prejudice and intolerance became widespread in the cultural sphere. It was in these stable times that my brothers and I were fortunate enough to spend the best years of our man-hood. Except for my eldest brother of course, whose life was terminated during the war by a pistol shot when he was twenty-one. You would have thought that we had

5

everything necessary to make us happy, but perhaps we lacked the ability to be happy, or were happy without knowing it, for we were beset by the family curse.

When this curse started, or whether it actually existed I cannot say for certain, but this much I know: my father's grandfather, who was very gifted and successful, fell on bad times. He possessed a remarkable ability to succeed and fail simultaneously.

He was born on a large farm up in northern Savolax, and when he had finished school, he got into a rowing-boat and rowed to Idensalmi, and from there he travelled to the capital of the Grand Duchy. To judge by the photographs we have he was not a stately man, he was short and thick-set, with a round face and small eyes, though photos don't tell us everything. There was obviously much more to him, for he succeeded in doing something quite unusual, he married an upper-class Swedish girl. Her maternal grandfather was an archbishop, and moreover the first man to be an archbishop in Finland,* and consequently the only one who counts, and is never forgotten.

She gave birth to two children and then died of pulmonary tuberculosis.

He worked his way up to a Ph.D. and began to fight for the rights of the Finnish language in Finland. Under Russian domination the situation was preposterous for you got nowhere unless you spoke Swedish and adopted the Swedish form of your name. This he would not do, but instead founded the first daily newspaper in Finnish and began to publish books in the language as well, which he printed in his own printing house. A pioneer undertaking of fantastic proportions that made him many enemies, even among those who were fighting for the same cause.

* Tengström, Johan Jacob, 1755–1832. Became Archbishop of Abo in 1817.

6

His home was burnt down, and the ship bringing machinery for his printing business was lost at sea. When he was accused of making a fortune at the expense of the ignorant Finns he abandoned his newspaper and his printing business and committed himself to a lunatic asylum where he died a very unhappy man. But his countrymen remember him today as the man who started the first newspaper in Finnish, which is far worthier than being the owner of a whole newspaper and publishing business. He succeeded in being first, but that was his bad luck.

My father's father was a happy man. All who remember him agree unanimously about that. He succeeded with everything he undertook. He never attempted anything at which he might have failed. It was said that he could have been the greatest painter in the land, but he didn't believe it. He said that he did not want to add to the number of mediocre artists, so he became a professor of the history of art. The first, of course, the only one who will never be forgotten.

When he was past seventy he was run over by a car, and thus became the first victim of a road accident in Brändö, the residential estate where he lived. That was a misfortune, but hardly an inherited family misfortune. It belongs rather to the category of pioneering exploits, the ability always to be first, which is also one of the curses of the family.

His father-in-law was a Colonel and the champion marksman of the Russian army. It is possible that his prominence in this art may have dimmed one part of my grandfather's happiness.

The Colonel had an irresistible desire to shine, and he wasn't satisfied by being a better shot than every single soldier in the whole of gigantic Russia. He wanted to be the best in the world and, in the absence of living competitors, he took to competing with the dead, even with sharpshooters who had never existed. He decided to surpass William Tell.

He forced his pregnant wife (I know nothing else about her, poor thing) to hold up a circular lead disc, half the size of a saucer, in her outstretched left hand, and then he shot through it from a distance of fifty metres. The bullet penetrated the disc almost exactly in the centre, and the Colonel had it framed behind glass. It still hangs on a wall in my childhood home.

My grandmother was born some months later without a left arm, and this extraordinary circumstance gave rise to a good deal of speculation, which worried the Colonel not a bit. He declared that he himself would at any moment be ready to sacrifice his right hand for such a masterly shot. I think it is probable that Grandmother and Grandfather would rather have kept Grandmother's arm than a lead disc, but, on the other hand, it is possible that Grandfather, who had a Finnish name, would not have been allowed to marry such a high-born Swedish girl if she had not had this little defect. In any case Grandmother's beauty was so great that the lack of an arm cannot have meant anything to Grandfather who had learnt to love the sculptures of antiquity, which lack both arms and legs.

Grandmother herself must have felt differently and, as the years passed, she isolated herself more and more, and her character took on some slightly bizarre features, which, while they may not have affected the happiness of their marriage, may have had a disastrous effect on the development of their only son. She became too protective, and begged and beseeched him not to make unnecessary trips into the town where he might be hit by falling tiles. Out of sheer defiance Father sought out the very place where tiles fall thickest, he became an architect.

Thereafter he never ceased to complain that he had

8

not been allowed to become what he wanted: an opera-singer. That was not sufficiently refined, he said. You see, he had become refined, much more refined than the farmer's son who had rowed to Idensalmi. And though it is true that refinement had been grafted on to the family before he came along, there wasn't enough of it to make him throw all refinement to the devil. Moreover, he realized that an opera-singer in a small country can't afford to buy a smart car or shoot clay pigeons. Worst of all an opera-singer stood on the stage and sang night after night while other people were enjoying themselves drinking champagne. In spite of his great interest in music Father was never able to sit out an opera beyond the end of the first act. He sang the second act at the Stock Exchange Club.

In the end he married the daughter of a sweet-manufacturer. She had beautiful dark eyes and a lot of money. He had culture and charm. After his grandfather had gone into the asylum at Lappviken, his father had been taken care of by the sister-in-law of our national poet Runeberg, and she was the archbishop's niece.

I have an enchanting photograph of my grandfather as a little boy sitting on the steps of Runeberg's veranda along with his little sister. Grandfather is sitting with one hand held firmly between his legs as if he intended that at least the life of future generations should be protected. Runeberg, adopting a patriarchal pose, is sitting on the veranda surrounded by the rest of his family, and looks like a person who does not keep count of how many children he has in his house. It was here that my grandfather began to work industriously in the stony patch of Finnish culture. In those days culture was more or less a family business, just as sweets were, and almost all the people engaged in it were related. Grandfather wrote several volumes of art history, and he became so well-known that one day his friend the composer Sibelius said to him: 'You are famous all over Europe, but damn it all, I'm famous in America too.'

At some stage in their lives the *nouveau riche* conceive the notion that they need culture and foolishly put their money into it. Of course they soon discover that culture is vanity and that money alone is enough to make people wise, beautiful, and well-educated.

Artistically gifted persons make another mistake. They believe that they can only fulfil themselves and be happy if they have enough money to make it unnecessary to think of inessentials. But with money their care-free existence gives them a surplus of time in which to reflect on how miserable man is by nature and, in order to forget their great unhappiness, they fling themselves into the hectic whirlpool of a life of pleasure, and then they become really unhappy. That is what happened to my father. No one knows what would have happened to his sweet wife, for she died when my twin brothers were born.

This was when my mother appeared on the scene. She was nineteen, and looked like a midsummer night beside a lake. My father believed that because she was beautiful she must be good. But my mother was not as good as she was beautiful, in actual fact she was so beautiful that she never bothered at all about being good.

But my father was very romantic, and he threatened to kill himself if she would not marry him. My mother, who was a provincial girl, was very flattered, especially since she had an exalted opinion of her own merits and never doubted that my father would keep his word. My father also had a very beautiful cabriolet, and he could frame his words in a way which had bowled over many a lady in Helsingfors and on the Continent. Typhus had taken his hair, and left him as bald as a billiard ball, but when he raised one eyebrow he looked demonic and exciting.

No one in the small town of Lahti looked exciting. My mother's father was the district medical officer, and her mother had matriculated and was a very wise woman. They both warned their daughter to postpone her marriage until after she had compieted her studies and become a qualified dentist. My father swore that his wife would never need to work. My mother did not think that a dentist's life would be particularly thrilling. When she heard that my father employed a nanny, a cook, and a housemaid, she decided to sacrifice herself for the sake of his three motherless children, and at the same time to save them from becoming fatherless. They married and this was the first but not the last time that Mother did a good deed which greatly contributed to the ruin of a human life.

They had a very beautiful home on two floors of a house. My father was an expert interior decorator and, thanks to this accomplishment, which was by no means common amongst architects, he was employed to fit out the home of Mannerheim, the White General, at Brunnspark. He did so to the General's great satisfaction. This man, who had delivered his country from socialism, often considered that the Finnish people were unworthy of him, failing to value him highly enough in peacetime. In spite of this, he remained in his comfortable home and in due course became a Field Marshal and the President. So it is not remarkable that my mother was fascinated by my father's gifts as an interior decorator. He also dressed her with exquisite taste, and hung upon her expensive but not ostentatious jewellery. My mother became even more beautiful and my father loved her not only as his wife, but also as his creation. It gave him great pleasure to show her off before the envious glances of his friends.

The strange thing about my father is, that, though he was a past master at handling fire-arms, cars, and boats, he never learnt how to treat women. With them he became involved in hazardous shots, collisions, and ignominious ship-wrecks because he never ceased to be amazed that they did not function as they should when he pressed the trigger, trod on the brake, or hauled in the sheet. He took some comfort from Strindberg's misogyny and Papini's disillusioned view of life, thinking that possibly only a tragic life was worth living. He set his camera on automatic release and took a picture of himself with his eyebrow raised unusually high. He pasted this picture on to a piece of cardboard and printed under it in elegant black letters 'The Devil's Friend'.

My mother was rather shocked. The devil had not been regarded as a friend in her home. She often looked at the picture, and the eyes in it had a hypnotic effect. She began to believe that he really was the devil's friend. It was the duty of every right-minded person to fight the devil and his followers. Betraying the devil's friend could not be regarded as a sin.

At any rate, not if one did it with a government minister.

But before she got as far as this she spent two years being a loving mother to my brothers. Father used to put the three boys with their mournful brown eyes into the bed beside her, and then he photographed them.

My eldest brother had a very violent temper as a child, he screamed and fought for no reason, and so my paternal grandmother, who lived in the flat under ours, had to take charge of him. One twin brother was a bed-wetter and the other ate wallpaper, and consequently the children were not allowed in Mother's bed very often. But nannies in those days were trustworthy and good-tempered, and my brothers were not neglected.

Father loved Mother's figure almost as much as she did herself. Her small, firm breasts were their common pride. You might have thought that the fashions of the Twenties had been made specially for her. Skirts were short and she had the prettiest legs in town, even a cavalry captain of Nyland's dragoons said so. When the old fellows – from my mother's point of view the gentlemen of the Stock Exchange Club were old fellows – looked at her their mouths watered, and it made my father happy to think that she was so desirable, but decidedly unhappy when he saw the effect this discovery had on her.

Party succeeded party and they made merry all night long, so that my brothers were seldom troubled by their parents. In so far as I cropped up in my parents' thoughts at this time they regarded me as a threat to her pretty breasts and as a prospective and tiresome interruption to their merry-making. Nevertheless, my fated approach loomed large. Frantic love-making has a way of getting children mixed up with love.

Of course I have only second-hand reports of this period and they are thoroughly untrustworthy, because I have got them from people who, in one way or another, were involved in my parents' life. My mother's sister, for instance, who had to pay for Mother's discarded gowns, speaks with some bitterness of her meanness and egotism. On the other hand Mother's beautiful but impecunious friend Greta, who got them for nothing, thinks that she had a generous nature. From these two reports one can possibly draw the conclusion that my mother was capricious and extremely unfair. This description merges with her character as well as a grain of sand merges with a beach. She was that and much more besides. . . .

When I look through old newspapers I soon see that at the time of my entry into the world there was prohibition in the republic of Finland. This did not prevent my being begotten in an agreeable state of moderate intoxication which gave my mother's innocent eyes a singularly sinful expression. This, combined with her

13

youth, was enough to drive even eminently prudent men of good upbringing to ill-considered deeds. My father was not prudent though he had been well brought up (brought down he called it, the old wag), and he was passionate and highly imaginative. My mother told me that he thrust a wooden penis into her. She told me this to make me understand how bestial he was, and that marriage with him was impossible. I do not have much sympathy with her argument as I have myself whittled and sand-papered a similar apparatus which I later used with pleasure and success in my own happier marriage.

Anyway, I have reason to think that she did not object to the treatment as much as she said. It frequently became apparent that, whatever she might say, she never again encountered a lover as versatile as my father, and that pleases me. He was after all my father, alas he was.

She also told me that he had used a vice to hold her wrist while he copulated with a whore he had brought home from the town. She was forced to look on and thought this was decidedly unattractive.

Why he had done it she did not say. It might have been tit for tat. I can assert with satisfaction that my father was a pioneer of group sex. It is not without pleasure that I have followed in his footsteps.

Where my parents stood politically at this time is not in any doubt. The Civil War was just over and the Russian princes whom my father had met while studying in Germany were now taxi-drivers and waiters in Paris. That told you plainly where socialism would lead you.

My mother's first lover of any importance was an aristocratic politician from the Liberal Party. He was so immoderately rich that he regarded himself as a liberal, and swore that no peasants had been shot on his estate.

Possibly my father sometimes felt sorry for the red devil. One of his friends, the author Jarl Hemmer, had made life difficult for himself by acquiring a social conscience at a time when a bank-book was the only book that mattered.

But no, it is just as impossible for me to give a fair picture of my parents from this period as from a later period. My experience of them is so totally subjective that everything I say about them can be regarded, purely and simply, as lies and fiction. This also applies to my brothers and myself. I could just as well tell you about Odysseus as if he were my brother. I don't believe for a moment that Penelope was faithful during the years her husband was absent. I'm sure that a hell of a lot of fucking went on at Ithaca, and that was right and proper. Devil take the old hypocrite Homer.

I will give you an example of my untrustworthiness as a witness. At the time my father died I thought he was a scoundrel and my mother (almost) an angel. Later on when she died I thought the reverse.

Now I just feel tremendously sorry for the lot of us.

2

In the year we went to Paris, my father was a marksman in the Finnish team at the Olympics. He had already come fourth in the clay pigeon shooting at the World Championship trials in Berlin. His chances of winning a medal in the Olympic Games should have been good. But he didn't win one, I do not know why.

It may have been because Father drank half a bottle of champagne after every fifteenth pigeon. There was no prohibition in France.

On our way there we travelled for part of the time in General Mannerheim's car. Mother said that he was very chivalrous but terribly boring.

Father never said anything about that journey, perhaps because he did not win a medal. He also thought it embarrassing that whenever he was drunk Mannerheim came up and thanked him for the way he had furnished and decorated his house. While he was about it he might have given Father a medal. Finland's White Rose was the only honour Father ever received for his services in promoting the already prevalent enthusiasm for marksmanship in the country. Our volunteer corps practised shooting at targets that represented soldiers of the Soviet Union with red stars in their woollen caps. Father never shot at an enemy though there is a story that he stood on his balcony and shot at Red guards. But that won't wash. Had he done so he would undoubtedly have killed some of them, for he could hit a bounding hare. Into the bargain the only balcony at home was a simple kitchen-balcony half a flight down, and Father would never have stood on that. Anyhow, when he wanted to hurt people he used subtler means than bullets.

My predicament was the opposite of theirs. I was on the way to being born which was the reason that I was allowed to go with them to Paris and my brothers were not. I also got champagne after every fifteenth pigeon, and it is just possible that, because Mother shared Father's tribulations so loyally, I was saved from being born prematurely in the Champs-Elysées. A suitcase fell on her stomach in the bus and without the soothing effects of alcohol on the muscles of her womb who knows what might have happened.

I don't myself believe that my life was saved by champagne, for when her time came Father had to drive Mother up and down a bumpy road in Sörnäs for an entire afternoon to get her pains going at all. On the other hand my embryonic drunkenness may have laid the foundations for alcoholism, who knows?

My birth was of course fantastically dramatic. I ought really to be very grateful to Mother that I was born at all. She never forgot to remind me of the fact, even under circumstances in which there seemed to be no reason whatever for being grateful one was alive.

The doctor had said that the mother might die when the child was born. Mother could choose. Herself or the child. She chose to risk her life and I was born and mother and child survived. The first person I saw was Dr Edvard Björkenheim, and had I been capable of understanding anything I should have heaved a sigh of relief at realizing that I had been born into Swedish-Finnish society where want was hardly known.

Into the bargain it is quite possible that Mother confused herself with Father's first wife, who had really died when the twins were born. She often considered the smallest particle of truth to be enough. If one wife

17

of Father's had died another might very well do so too. However that may be, I was born which was more than my younger brother or sister succeeded in being, in spite of the fact that his or her papa was a man who had dedicated his life to the struggle for justice, if not to equality. And the papa in question was of course not my father, who only happened to be married to my mother.

But Mother never talked about that. Nevertheless, she managed to make her abortion appear to have been a sacrifice. In this case, for the man she loved so deeply that she did not want to ruin his career. Thus this unborn child did not destroy anything but my parents' marriage, and the child itself was spared from ever knowing what a mess love can make of things.

I do not believe for a moment that Mother really loved the child's father. She was always complaining about his bad breath. The woman he was married to accused him of smelling like a stable, it was only politically that he had the right odour.

His passionate love letters, in which he implored Mother to flee with him, were among the documents she left. It might have been Count Sparre of the ballad writing to Elvira Madigan, but Mother was not a circus artiste and her lover was only a lord. So they never fled anywhere, a little child was never born, and a great man remained great.

This meant that he was left without heirs, and when he died he bequeathed all his millions to a fund for the promotion of Swedish-Finnish culture. As a result I finally got a fraction of the fortune which I might have inherited in part, if his breath had not been bad.

When his scholarships were being distributed, his widow exclaimed loudly: 'Is that man to be given money? He's a Finn!' On my way from the platform I stopped in front of her bowing humbly as Finns should and said: 'Thanks for the coppers and for the sweets.'

Her pride prevented her from appreciating the fact that I was not only thanking her for the money, but also for the innumerable boxes of sweets that her husband had given me by way of compensation for the happy childhood of which he imagined he had deprived me.

And indeed, how happy we might have been in our beautiful home. Not so long ago I had occasion to visit it. One of my friends lives there now and it all looks different, but when I walked through the rooms I remembered everything as it had been.

I remembered the wolf that stood panting behind the curtains in the nursery at night and which fled as soon as a grown-up came into the room, summoned by my terrified cries.

In the dining-room my father chased my mother brandishing a chair and I threw myself between them. I am filled with horror when I think of it. That memory has no beginning and no end. Only the raised chair and my screams.

The bullet holes are still there in the wooden floor of the attic where my father shot at the green devils who were attacking him. My mother's sister, whose bottle of Eau de Cologne he had drunk, thought he was trying to shoot her and, along with the housemaid, took refuge behind the side-board in the dining-room. No one was hurt.

The blood on the walls of the boys' room had gone of course. There was new wallpaper. There had probably been a dozen new layers, but I still thought I could see the stains on the wall if I shut and opened my eyes quickly.

In the room beside it an angel had appeared to my father's mother. He stood beside her bed for so long that she felt that she too must get out of bed and stand beside him. They never spoke a word to each other. The angel only smiled kindly.

Gone was the dark cell where we children had to sit if we had been naughty. It was a hole under the stairs where the dirty linen was kept. The built-in cupboard for prizes, with its painted glass door that I had kicked to pieces, was also gone. I had stood waiting impatiently to go out with my parents who were dawdling, and had kicked the door which was not made of wood as I thought, but of glass that fell clattering to the floor. It was like desecrating a shrine, and I expected a frightful punishment, which I well deserved. But both Father and Mother said it didn't matter, and that incident upset my sense of values for ever. What is sacred in this world? The friend who now lives there has installed a lavatory in its place.

I was born on a Sunday and Sunday's child is happy and easy-going, and everything turns out well for him. My father was very proud of me and so was my mother. She said I was a very sensitive child and caught colds easily. Consequently, when I went out I was always muffled up like an Arctic explorer.

As it turned out it was for this very reason that I so often caught colds. After my parents were divorced and I was sent to live with my mother's parents in Forssa I seldom had one. They peeled off most of my clothes and said that feeling a bit cold was healthy.

But I wonder if my soul wasn't cold too, for I longed for my brothers and our dog, and my mummy and my daddy and our cook, who was called Ida.

3

My first five years were actually only an extension of my nine months in my mummy's tummy. They too are without memories, and I cannot be sure whether what I remember happened then or later or if I've only been told about it.

Mummy's tummy was of course more shock-proof than was my childhood home.

The safe place was the shawl that my paternal grandmother wore over her shoulders, and the long skirt that came down to her ankles like a sturdy pillar. She had white hair.

Mother had very short skirts, you could see her knees. I was attracted to the smile on her face. And I wasn't the only one.

The scent of Father's cigar.

The smell of leather and petrol in the car.

The rustle of the wind through the leaves of the trees in the park.

The dog's fur.

Sitting on a warm stone in the forest sensuously holding in check the pressure on my guts. Then, at a safe distance, I could see lions and tigers in the thickets.

When I waded out into deep water by the steamship's landing-stage and was near to drowning, but found I could swim by moving my arms and holding my panic in check.

To hold my panic in check all the time. Sooner shit in my pants.

The clay pigeon that broke to pieces in the air and Father hitting the largest bit with his second shot. I was proud of that.

We scorched live lizards in the forest by placing them in a ring of burning twigs. They rushed hither and thither and finally jumped into the flames and curled up horribly. This sacrifice to unknown gods filled me with remorse and gave me a bad conscience which remained in my heart like the flame on the grave of the unknown soldier.

The hatred I felt for my brothers when they pulled to pieces the toy car my parents had brought me from England. Their parents had not brought them toy cars that I could pull to pieces. I discovered injustice as the propertied classes see it.

When Father was angry with me he hit the twins. Injustice was clearly more appropriate for some people than for others.

Father hit my brothers, but I knew that he would never hit me.

Once during the war I was given a hard blow on the back of my neck in a dark doorway. I never saw the person who hit me. I have never been hit by anyone I could look in the eye. This surprises me for I think I am just the sort of person anyone would be pleased to hit. My head is pear-shaped, like a punch-ball, and my ridiculously aristocratic nose looks as if it were begging to be bashed in. But clearly I haven't the right caste-mark on my forehead to attract blows.

This reminds me of Father and Abrahamsson's bull. They met in a field and the bull had a dreadful reputation for being dangerous. The bull knew nothing of Father's reputation and it went fearlessly into the attack. They were far from being matched in weight. Father weighed barely seventy kilos and the bull nearer four hundred, I should think. Father saw the bull coming but walked on to meet it without moving a muscle of his face. A metre away from Father the bull stopped and snorted. Father's eyebrow shot up to the heights and he walked on staring the bull fixedly in the eyes. The bull took a step backwards and glared wildly, then another step, and then retired step by step. And so they crossed the field, Father forwards, the bull backwards.

I saw this display of courage from the safe side of the fence, and when my uninjured father came up to me I thought he would comment upon the incident in some way, but he didn't. The bull of course could not do so and Father was always fair. He was that unfashionable thing, a gentleman, which was, I believe, one of the reasons for his misfortunes.

My maternal grandfather, on the other hand, was a man of honour which was and is a much more common phenomenon in our barren land. So far as I know he was always just, incorruptibly honest, reliable, and unable to understand people who were not.

He was well over six foot and wore pince-nez. His back was as straight as a ruler. He did not even move his head when, during the siege of Lahti in the Civil War, a bullet grazed the back of his neck and ploughed into the head of the German officer walking beside him up Station Street Hill.

He had no sympathy for the Reds. He thought people should do an honest job of work, not make revolutions. He valued the punctuality of the trains in Mussolini's Italy and Hitler's Germany more than democracy, and he and I rejoiced together over Franco's successes in the Spanish Civil War.

Grandfather knew everything and what he did not know could be found in Meyer's encyclopaedia of which he had a leather-bound copy on his shelves. He used to tell me about the stars and the moon, which moved as punctually as Hitler's trains. He also told me of the incurable diseases of stupidity, laziness and wickedness. He did not believe in neuroses. When a hysterical lady sent for him he cured her by slapping her bare buttocks with a wet towel. From being the scourge of the medical profession in Lahti with her hysterics, she never again summoned a doctor on that account. Grandfather thought that this entitled him to a first class degree in psychiatry which, by the way, he called nonsense.

In the summers he took me out fishing in the archipelago. I rowed while he sat in the stern and studied the topography of the seabed through the limpid water. We wound round rocks and sandbanks like a dog who is going to lie down, before he cast anchor in exactly the right spot. Then we pulled out one perch after another until we had the whole shoal in the creel behind the stern.

The harbour-master at Kyrkbacken, who knew of Grandfather's luck, used to go to the spots where we fished. But he must have cast anchor a few centimetres out, for he never caught half as many fish as we did. It was heavy work rowing back with all the perch trailing behind us in the creel. Grandfather gave the whole catch to the boarding-house where we were staying. While we were there the only dish offered was fish soup and possibly our fellow guests were not too fond of him. That did not worry him, for he regarded men under six feet tall as drips, which most people in this poverty-stricken country were at that time. Females did not register at all, so great peace reigned on the heights where his pince-nez glittered in the sun like a lighthouse. He did not even take them off when swimming.

He used to lie on his back in the water some distance from the shore with his glasses on his nose, his hands behind his head, and his legs crossed. Though he was as thin as a lath he floated like a nylon rope, and he could actually lie and sleep like that for half an hour.

Cheeky outboard-motors didn't disturb the peace of the archipelago in those days, and it was only when he began to feel cold that he woke up and came ashore.

When I pinched my finger in a car door and, so far as I remember, it was right off and lost for good, Grandfather pieced it together again so skilfully that after a short time I couldn't show the scar to my friends and very soon forgot which finger it was. That was when I decided to become a doctor like Grandfather.

In spite of the fact that he was condescending towards women, Grandfather was a bit afraid of Grandmother. She had to go to some lengths to make it appear that he was master of the house, which was essential if he was to be respected as the district medical officer and chairman of Lahti town council. It was also a necessity for Grandmother that he should seem to be in control, for otherwise she might have been accused of marrying a mouse of a man because she could not get anything better. And, as I knew that he was not only the tallest of men but the best, I could not help being impressed by Grandmother of whom he stood in some awe.

He only dared to bring out the whisky bottle when she was away, and then he used to lie on the sofa in his consulting-room and hum 'Chin chin Chinaman'.

As I had a father who was not afraid of bulls, and a Grandfather who was not afraid of anything except Grandmother, and a grandmother who was not afraid at all (so far as I know she believed in God), it is not surprising that I learned to value most highly the thing I most lacked, courage.

It was not long before I became bold enough to give up attempting to demonstrate my courage and openly confessed that I was afraid. Afraid of most things.

4

What is it that forms a child? The happy or the unhappy
moments? If a child only remembers the happy moments
it is perhaps because they were so few, and then we
may well say that its childhood was unhappy, or vice
versa.

People talk of happy childhood, happy old age, and a
happy marriage. This is surely because as concepts they
are the most empty. When nothing happens all is well.

I don't know whether some of the events I remember
from my childhood were happy or unhappy, but they
have remained with me like the birthmarks on my skin.

Once in Forssa I was hanging on my grandmother's
arm when we tumbled over in the middle of the market-
place. That I remember this incident so vividly must be
due to the fact that I experienced its social dimensions
through Grandmother. In a little place like Forssa, served
only by a narrow gauge railway from Humppila, also an
insignificant place, it was quite unthinkable that the
medical officer's wife should lie flat on her stomach in
the market-place.

Of course it is possible that there were other reasons
why we moved to Lahti immediately afterwards, and I
went to Miss Härkman's infant school.

Memories multiply from this point.

The Oljas, who lived under us, had bed bugs. It was
fascinating to see them sucked out of the inside of the
bed, to march in close formation into the triumphal arch
of the hungry vacuum-cleaner. They looked like soldiers

in splendid uniforms and they marched to their death as soldiers always do. But it did not help matters and the bugs in Mr and Mrs Olja's beds were never ending.

People told me that many reds were shot in the concentration camp in Lahti during the civil war. But they told it in such a way that I felt no pity. Though so many were killed, innumerable poor people remained whose lives were, with good reason, unendurable, above all to themselves.

According to Grandfather the world had endless supplies of everything. It had limitless quantities of coal and oil, and in Finland there were the forests, her green gold. It was only because Father was stupid that he had lost his money. He had invested it the wrong way.

My father was a drip, Grandfather said.

Fortunately my father belonged to a social class where you did not become poor just because you lost your money. But he was obliged to retrench, and he felt this more than those who had nothing to retrench with. The hardest part is not losing your money but losing your rich friends.

My mother's parents had always been economical and they continued to save even after it was no longer necessary. In fact saving gave them so much satisfaction that they had no need of extravagance to make them happy. But unfortunately, well-to-do people's thrift may be as merciless in its effects as rich people's extravagance, it invariably harms the children and the dispossessed.

One day, when all my stockings turned out to be undarned, I was sent to school in Grandmother's silk stockings, which were in good repair, but much too big. Everyone could see that I was wearing ladies' stockings, and if I had not succeeded in beating Heikki Mustakallio at wrestling in the break, I should probably have lost my self-respect for ever. And that, as far as I can see, is the same as losing your freedom. And without freedom life is worthless. Every child in Finland must learn that. But they don't necessarily learn what freedom is, for if they did their eagerness to give their lives for freedom might diminish, and that would not be good for our defences.

I had a friend whose ancestor had saved the king. In the heat of battle he had given his horse to the king, who had escaped to safety. He himself lost his life, but the king was one of the grateful variety, and had ennobled him posthumously. My friend was very proud of his ancestor.

My maternal Grandfather's ancestors had been pirates in Gotland, and they never gave the king anything, but instead stole as much from him as they could. They did what they wanted, whereas my friend's ancestor did what the king wanted. I had no difficulty in deciding which of them was the more independent and free.

5

Our pirate blood showed itself in many ways. My grandfather was a man of honour, but he had a sword-stick, a walking-stick in which a sword was hidden. In his youth he had punched holes with it in a number of signboards in the town where he later became chairman of the town council. More than this the pirate blood did not demand, and subsequently he was an irreproachable supporter of social order, so far as I know.

Among the progeny of my ancestors there are bank directors, engineers, business men and farmers and, to tell the truth, it has been exceedingly difficult to find anything exciting about them. It is almost certain that the pirates were ordinary farmers in Gotland who, by a quirk of history, were allotted an unexpected and adventurous role.

They supplied the king, who was besieged in Stockholm, with provisions. In the king's eyes they were patriots, but in the eyes of the besiegers they were pirates. They just wanted to sell their wares, preferably to the highest bidder, and the king, who had no fields or barns in the city which he could rob, paid the best. The king was Albreckt of Mecklenburg, and the besieger Queen Margareta of Denmark. She had no need of provisions, and when she was victorious the Brotherhood of Victuallers lost their position as purveyors to H.M. the King and were made outlaws instead. But even as pirates they preserved their honest, steadfast spirit which sprouted from the same soil as the turnips and cucumbers they cultivated. With the passing of the centuries they became well-adjusted middle-class people, who were prepared to commit all the historical follies of the middle-classes. All except Grandfather's younger brother, Veikko. You could see from his dress that he was Tolstoyan, for although he was a qualified land surveyor he sauntered about barefoot on his property at Somero with a fur cap askew on his head. Like the Generals in free Finland he wore his fur cap in winter and summer, but he had very little use for Generals or other persons in authority. It is likely that he did not approve of the mass extermination of peasants and Red guards, and he said that pigs, and cows, and sheep made far fewer mistakes than men. They were born with the wisdom life demands, but man was born with stunted instincts and an empty head. A head it was easy to fill with all the accumulated stupidities that his brother (my grandfather) had on his bookshelves – bound in pigskin.

A dog could pee a message on a post by the wayside, and another dog could read it, but human beings could not even understand the words they themselves had shaped so carefully. As examples my grandfather's brother let fall words such as tolerance, equality, freedom, and love. All of them served as good excuses for oppression, exploitation, war, and hatred. And if a man peed on a flower, that flower died, so poisonous and unfit for nature had man become.

Consequently, Veikko preferred talking to animals. But as he had a hot temper he often fell to quarrelling with them too. He could stand beside the pigsty and scold the pigs for fifteen minutes because, though they had the wisdom of pigs, they did not always understand what their master expected of them. Veikko was a gigantic man, well over six foot tall, but when he was angry his voice rose to a squeak, very unsuitable in the offspring of a pirate. Moreover he always addressed the things he was scolding as 'you there'.

'Now then, now then, you there. What are you up to, you there?' he would bellow at a hog which was altogether too eager to get to the trough. But he never called it 'you pig', for when a human being calls anyone a pig he means it to be insulting, and though Veikko could be furious with a pig he would never insult it.

He only quarrelled with the people he loved. During the last twenty years of his life he never spoke to his wife. He said what he had to say to her through the children, though they were all in the same room. His marriage was no happier than Leo Tolstoy's, and in this too he was a genuine Tolstoyan. Most of all he hated doctors. His brother was a doctor. When, at eighty, he fell ill with pneumonia and a doctor was called, he pushed a cupboard up against the bedroom door, and would not let him in. He managed to hold out until death rescued him from the danger of medical treatment.

I thought that was worthy of an old pirate.

Every year, as soon as school was finished in the early summer, I was sent to Somero where I had to stay until Grandfather's summer holiday began and we could go to the archipelago. To me the weeks at Somero were like being banished to a slave-camp.

Veikko's philosophy of life was that everyone must work from dawn to dusk, no one was too small. I remember arable land that stretched as far as the horizon, where I crept along in scorching sunshine pulling out weeds from endless strips. I remember hay that had to be hung on millions of poles, I remember manure that had to be spread over the whole earth. I remember ditches that had to be dug from Pitkäjärvi to the Caspian Sea, or at least to Lake Ladoga. Everything in the country was without end or meaning. No sooner had you pulled up a weed than it sprouted again.

31

And then there was frost.

As a child I was mortally afraid of frost. If it came there would be a bad harvest and we should all starve to death. Veikko preached that man must be one with nature, but what help was that when frost could come and destroy the foundations of man's existence? Nature concentrated her energies towards making short work of man. The frost took his crops, the moths his clothes. But neither frost nor moths could harm the cannon and bayonets which sprang up as rapidly as weeds. The whole of life was a struggle against a superior power, whose forbearance was nowhere near as great as its animosity, so my grandfather's brother assured me.

When we were mending the roof of a barn a beam fell down and missed me by a hair's breadth. If it had hit me it would have crushed my head, and I should have died. It was perfectly obvious that because inanimate objects lacked any good will they must be possessed of active ill will. An object never undertook a good deed on its own, but on the other hand you were liable to be attacked by bloodthirsty odds and ends of all sorts. The only thing one had on one's side was luck, and I knew for certain that luck had saved me. On that day I made a pact with luck, for even if luck was unreliable it was the only thing in which a human being could put his trust.

My maternal grandparents hoped that I should grow strong and healthy among the peasants, and I certainly did, so much so that my vigour nearly cost me my life.

Grandmother took my close shave as a hint that I ought to be baptized, though this was against my father's wishes. Father was the devil's friend and, correct as he was, he thought that to enter into a compact with his opponent was improper. But Grandmother, who had seen where Father's unsuccessful monetary speculations had led him, was not convinced that he would be any better at managing souls. According to her, there would be

32

considerably less risk in living as a Christian, than in dying as a heathen.

She therefore took me to the parson and asked him to baptize me on the spot. No one asked me what I thought about it and I very nearly melted away with shame when I had to go through a ceremony intended for the newly born. I should have liked to bite the parson's hand when he poured water on my head, and gave me the name I had had all my life. I thought it was absurd, but Grandmother was happy, and I always liked to please her as I loved her.

In return I begged to be allowed to give up going to Somero where all kinds of dangers threatened an inexperienced city boy, and Grandmother, who saw that it would be too cynical to regard baptism as a sufficient protection against accidents, agreed. The following summer I was sent instead to a Christian boys' camp, near Hangö. There I learned to masturbate and had a surprising success.

6

I had not been more than two days at the Christian summer camp before I was longing for Somero. Military discipline and a destructive spirit of competition were the rule here. You must always be first and best if you wanted to be worth a tinker's curse, and as only one at a time could be first and best the rest of us were mostly not worth a tinker's curse.

I felt very degraded when I discovered that I had been infected by the general eagerness to curry favour with the parsons who were our leaders. One was hearty and the other was handsome. The handsome one said that a man never complained when he got soap in his eyes. I got soap in my eyes in the sauna and I did not complain, though it smarted so horribly that it nearly killed me. But the parson did not notice. Because I didn't complain.

We marched in line and the parsons shouted commands like 'dress' and 'dismiss', to make good soldiers of us. The clergy in Finland have always had a soft spot for the military as they realize that no path to God's heaven is as direct as a soldier's. Drill welded us together into a typically military group where everyone hates the commanding officers and suspects his fellows of doing the dirty work of those in authority. We took out our humiliation on God.

The more vehemently we succeeded in blaspheming when the parsons were not present the greater was our satisfaction. The peak of our protest was a masturbating orgy in which twenty boys sat in a ring and tossed each other off while singing a psalm. It was very uplifting and gave me the first hint of the diverse uses to which my cock could be put.

Though I had been told by Grandmother to sleep with my hands on the coverlet I had not realized that the little fellow could be used for other purposes than peeing. I still thought that children came into this world through the navel. I arrived at this conclusion on my own, for no one talked to me about such matters. Of course at Somero I saw piglets and calves being born, but even that didn't convey anything to me. Man was God's image, and the only confinement anyone had bothered to explain to me was the Virgin Mary's. Her manner of giving birth seemed to me nice and suitable for human beings. At that time I still thought that Mother was like a madonna.

But in God's own summer camp the truth about the whole shameful business dawned on me. Man came into the world via the same passages through which the body expels all its other refuse. Low passions dominated man and, in spite of God's exhortations and teachings, he continued to wallow in the dung out of which he had come into the world. That was why he had been driven out of paradise and put into a summer camp. When I realized what an instrument of the devil I carried between my legs I was filled with joy at having acquired a weapon I could use against oppression. I became an indefatigable masturbator.

Then came the miracle.

All the boys had been instructed to carve out of a block of wood a sailing-boat of a given size and design. All were successful except me.

My boat was somehow a bit crooked, and when I tried to correct the fault the boat shrank alarmingly in size. Everyone jeered at me and told me it would overturn and be incapable of sailing. The parsons joined in, obviously filled with malicious delight. I should have liked to burn my boat, but the parsons said that all the boats must take part in the big regatta with which the camp closed. Then our positions in order of precedence could be finally allocated, for our boats were driven by the Lord's wind and He would be our judge.

To show what a miserably low value I put on my sailing-boat I named her Lotta, the ugliest name I could hit on. When I released the boat I hoped that the first gust of wind would overturn her, so that my torment would be as brief as possible. The Lord's wind did indeed fill Lotta's sail, and the Lord's wave carried her steadily across the bay to the other bank where she arrived at least ten lengths ahead of any other boat. Lotta had won, I was given a certificate of merit, and the parsons said I was a model boy.

My grandparents were very pleased and proud of my success and said that the best thing in the world was a healthy spirit in a healthy body. I said I quite agreed with them, but added artfully that I did not much care for the indecent goings on at the camp. I was obliged to be more explicit and my grandmother was very upset, and said that I must never go there again. Grandfather took down a medical book from his shelves in which it said that those who masturbate go mad, develop a disease of the spinal cord, become impotent, and are unhappy for the rest of their lives.

I did not want to go mad, nor did I want to become impotent, though I did not know what the word meant. I therefore decided to give up tossing myself off, so I crept down under the bed-clothes and concluded my sinful life with a couple of extra good goes.

I did this night after night while, bit by bit, my feelings of guilt gnawed like hungry rats at my strength of will. I realized that I was hopelessly lost and that, even before I had reached the age of twelve, I had no future.

My intensive masturbating also tired me out to such an extent that I was unable to learn my German grammar properly.

All the same it was in a German book entitled *Wie bist du Weib?** that I found my salvation. That book was also on Grandfather's shelves, but he had not given it to me. I found it myself and studied it in order to discover what I was going to be cheated of as the result of an untimely demise. But in that book it said that masturbation was quite natural, and that all normal children did it. A stone fell from my heart and I celebrated the event with a real set to.

Nevertheless masturbation had harmed me. I had lost confidence in my strength of will. I had really tried to stop, but I had been unable to. It was also clear to me that my grandparents, in their wisdom, rated morals higher than truth, and that left me not knowing to which I should adhere.

In any case it was the end of slavery at Somero and at the boys' camp at Hangö. After that my summer holidays began at my father's house on Brändö.

* *What makes you a woman?*

7

Father had already got himself a new bride, of course. He was the steadfast type who would never dream of being unfaithful to anyone except his wife.

I have never been able to fathom the grounds on which he chose a wife, but one thing is certain, they were not good ones, for his choice never turned out really well. It is possible that he was such an incorrigible romantic that, whenever he fell in love, he immediately wanted to get married.

However, it was perfectly obvious that he had a strong partiality for very young girls. Innocence fascinated him, or maybe he thought that he would be able to mould a young girl to his requirements.

But his virgins were not made of tractable marble but of Finnish granite, and on them his hammer and chisel made no impression. It was the poor designer who grew crooked. And that happened this time too. The girl was young and beautiful, but she wasn't going to allow herself to be bullied. Besides, she was so very unintellectual that his *Weltschmerz* ran off her as water from a goose. It was no good being tragic with her, but he did not discover this in the first flush of love.

She did not come alone, she brought with her a parrot and her whole family. In addition to the parrot this consisted of a mother, impregnated with kindness, and numberless brothers and sisters, who would all have become millionaires if they had emigrated to America or Australia. As they had not done so they had plenty of time to visit our home and depress Father by their excellence. The kind mother sometimes stayed for weeks and called both the parrot and Father 'precious friend', which nearly drove him frantic.

Our new stepmother was not many years older than my eldest brother, but the task facing her did not cause her any qualms. You would have thought from the look of things that she had been appointed managing director of a business ripe for bankruptcy, for she energetically started to put everything to rights. Father did not want help, he wanted commiseration, and consequently it was not long before he developed an ambition to see her fail. He could not endure integrated people.

Father was justifiably disappointed with life which for him resembled the children's chute at the amusement park at Fiskertorp. The child was lifted on to a platform from where it steadily descended until it landed with a splash in the sea.

Everything good had happened to him before he was thirty. He had been rich, handsome, gifted, successful, carefree, popular, loved, envied, and young. And then suddenly he was pushed down from the platform, and it was no fun at all landing in the water.

It was not without justification that Father blamed his mother for spoiling him without making sure that it would be possible for him to live the life of a spoiled person in the future as well. But my grandmother had already transferred her care and attention to my eldest brother, with whom she was repeating the manœuvre.

Father had learnt by bitter experience that wealth which consists of a private fortune is not a thing in which to put your trust. At first your position is made pretty secure by the ramifications of a whole family's financial interests, for these can never be completely overtaken by depression and bad trade conditions. But Father had speculated and lost, and consequently his rich friends – who were still rich – thought he had let them down. People who lose their money are not dumb, but what they have to say is worthless. They have joined the grey ranks of the nondescript masses. The sweet factory also ceased to send us children their usual marzipan cake at Christmas.

The inhabitants of Brändö would have preferred to see Father remove himself from the island after he started to sell carpets at Stockmann's, even though he did it with a Havana cigar in his mouth. The residential estate had been built for educated Swedish-speaking persons of good family, who had no financial worries. In true Swedish-Finnish spirit they had entrenched themselves in a stronghold which shut out the increasingly unpleasant facts.

When the first poor, Finnish-speaking artisan succeeded in establishing himself on the estate it provoked deep gloom, and the day was at once envisaged on which the municipality would have to shoulder a social services tax. In order to avert this misfortune, the vicar was sent to offer the Finn a suitable gratuity if he would voluntarily decamp. He saw reason, accepted the money, and took his departure, never to return. The inhabitants of Brändö could breathe freely again and decided that in future they would never let poverty enter the community.

In fact everything on Brändö had been planned for happiness and beauty. The island had originally been bought by a company who wanted to build a model community on the English pattern. The architect, Bertil Jung, had drawn up a town plan for an Art Nouveau style of housing that looked like John Bauer's illustrations for the fairy-tale book, Dwarfs and Trolls. There were to be romantic brick castles with rose-gardens, and narrow, winding roads crossing the estate here and there. People were to live in a beautiful fairy-tale that ended with the words: 'and they all lived happily ever after.'

To tempt other rich and happy people from St. Petersburg and similar brilliant metropolises to take their holidays here, he built a casino, an hotel, indoor and outdoor tennis-courts, and a golf course. In order to make the community quite self-contained he also built a church, a school, and a fire-station, and laid out a cemetery on an idyllic little island close by. So there was no need to leave Brändö even when you died.

The vicar never came to us with a proposal that we should leave, for after all we were not entirely destitute, and moreover Brändö itself had not quite lived up to expectations.

In spite of the fact that the inhabitants had shut their eyes and tried to turn their backs on it, the First World War had broken out. The rich tourists, who should have come to the hotel, never came, and then there was prohibition, which paralysed the casino, and the depression, which put a stop to further development of the estate. Brändö had become the half-finished set for a fairy-tale, and in it Father found himself playing Hamlet.

The part suited him but not the audience. His new relatives were lower middle-class people who thought he had everything he needed. They found it impossible to understand that their plebeian assessment of his situation plunged him into the deepest need.

8

I had seen the world. I had been in Somero, and in Lahti, and in Forssa, and in the archipelago, but my brothers had never been anywhere.

They used to sit on the steps outside the house and guess the makes of cars. When they heard a car coming up the hill they guessed, and the one who guessed right won. But where the car came from or where it was going they could not tell.

When they were little they had been allowed to go with Father in his car to Degerö. But when the depression came the car was sold. One of the twins once went to Riihimäki by train, but he was travel-sick the whole way and never stopped vomiting.

Brändö was their world and they thought that the world was like Brändö.

They knew that the Russians were a pack of scoundrels and should be hated, with the exception of those Russians who managed the Green-White tennis-club on Brändö, for they were rich Russians who had fled from the Bolsheviks.

The groundsman at the tennis-club was also a Russian.

'Ov from court,' he would yell at us.

Because he yelled at us and because he was not rich you would have thought we might be allowed to hate him. But that was not so, for he was a faithful servant, and he too had fled from the Bolsheviks.

If they had only been able to, all the Russians in the

whole of Russia would have fled from the Bolsheviks, and then we should not have had to hate any of them. Very soon we should be helping them all to escape. That was why the members of the voluntary defence corps exercised on the golf course next to the tennis-courts.

Father was not a member of the defence corps but, on patriotic occasions, he wore his Olympic marksman's uniform. One Finn was equal to ten Russians, everyone knew that, and it couldn't be harder to hit a Russian than it was to hit a clay pigeon, and Father had hit ninety clay pigeons out of a hundred. Consequently he was equal to ten Finns, but he would not get mixed up in politics.

Toffy's father was Father's best friend and they were in the habit of drinking quantities of cognac together. Toffy's father was an artist and had designed his own house. It looked as if, when on a visit to Italy, he had drawn a picture of some house there, and subsequently had had a similar house built on Brändö from his drawing. He had clearly only drawn the outside of the house, for the inside wasn't as good, and it was really rather a tiresome place to live in.

To show Toffy's papa how much he liked and valued him Father deposited his pistol with him. He did this to prevent himself from committing suicide when he was low. Of course at the same time he promised Toffy's papa that he would not use any of the other twenty firearms he had in his gun cupboard at home.

Some days later Toffy's parents drove into the river at Borgå and were drowned because the inhabitants of Borgå couldn't be bothered to fish people out of the river who didn't belong. Toffy, who was an only child, inherited his mother's fortune and his father's artistic temperament. He became enormously rich.

Father only lost his money some years after this, so you might say that he and Toffy's father parted friends.

But after he lost it we boys could no longer play with Toffy, as we had lost so much more than he had.

The poor orphan was obliged to suppress the intellectual inclinations he had inherited from his impecunious father in order to come to terms with the money he had inherited from his mother. His rich relations suspected that he was a good-for-nothing like his father, who only painted pictures. To prove the contrary he became a shipowner to whom the Korean War was a great blessing. He earned vast sums of money on freights and soon dreamed of the day when he would invite the shipowners Gustav Thordén and Sven Salén to dinner in order to hear them say: 'And what is your opinion, Toffy?'

But you can't put your trust in war, and just when things were at their best it came to an end and so did the profits. Toffy's money ran into the sea as if someone had opened the sea-cocks in his ships. Within a short time he was ruined. Family, friends, and wives (he'd picked them up on Brändö, of course), turned their backs on him, and there he stood with nothing left but the gifts he had inherited from his father, which all the Cassandras had prophesied would be his downfall.

At fifty Toffy had a rapid academic career and created out of nothing the country's Maritime Museum. This brought him such renown that Aristotle Onassis himself would have felt honoured if he had been able to say: 'And what is your opinion, Toffy?'

You would have thought that this would have reinstated him, but that is not what happened. A man who has lived on Brändö is for ever branded with the false values of sham reality. Without money he was nothing, in fact as far as the inhabitants of Brändö were concerned he did not exist. To show them his disdain, without succumbing to socialism or other vulgar forms of radicalism, he hung pictures of Nicholas II and his family on his walls and proclaimed aloud that life in Finland

44

lost its meaning when the Romanoffs were driven from the throne.

His attitude may appear rather grotesque, but actually it was not. The upper-class in a small country is always served by tyranny, which hurts the people but upholds the privileges of the rich. The Tsar's police are much to be preferred to the police of the landowners or the big bosses, and independence is a middle-class illusion which has led to much confusion and reification. As things stood gentlemen were obliged to raise their hats to people who had themselves worked to get their money. Toffy wanted to emphasize that money without traditions and fine manners is a mere nothing, even if life without money is hardly worth half as much.

Certainly Brändö was a classless society where some were more equal than others.

Toffy wasn't the only person who grew to resemble his surroundings. They were fatal for our country's greatest sculptor, Wäino Aaltonen. They, and the sad fact that Father's financial predicament had forced him to let a room to the former wife of one of my new step-mother's many brothers.

Wäino Aaltonen, whose studio was on Brändö, met her at our house. He was a friend of ours, and as early as the Twenties had made a magnificent portrait med-allion of my paternal grandfather. Father had ordered a plaster copy of the same size, and had it built into the open fireplace on the first floor.

Stepmother's former sister-in-law was an enchanting woman, who looked as if she had once posed for Renoir. She never had, the bloom of her youth had been shared between three rubbishy husbands, and she wanted to plant her luxuriant maturity in fertile soil.

Wäino Aaltonen looked upon her with delight, and said that he loved women whose thighs were as thick as buckets. He was famous for his primeval strength and his sculptures seemed on the point of exploding. She realized that if this strength could be combined with upper-class Swedish-Finnish culture the result must be incomparable art. At the turn of the century her father had belonged to Nyland's Yachting Club, and he had never been niggardly with the punch when afloat. Culture and education were what Wäino lacked, and these things she could give him.

It was not long before they married and he became a professor and an academic and she succeeded in remoulding him to comply with the dignity of his new position. Not a single day of national festivity passed on which he did not embellish the proceedings with his noble presence, and she regarded him as her own handiwork. She received much praise for having turned an old wrestler into a cultural personality. The Amalgamated Nordic Bank began to buy everything he produced, his art had certainly become very cultivated.

It was clear that, even if he possessed primeval strength, her strength was much greater, and she might justifiably have signed the statues of the presidents outside the Parliament Buildings, or the greater number of the anaemic bronze figures in the Nordic Bank. Everyone is now at liberty to view the works of art resulting from this magnificent trial of strength as either victory or defeat.

The inhabitants of Brändö were not particularly impressed by their great artist and no work of his is on public display on the island. But this is not suprising as the sculptor Matti Haupt lived on Brändö too. His wife was very rich and they lived in one of the largest and grandest villas. You only needed to look at their house to see who was the greater artist.

It was pretty much the same in the case of President Ståhlberg. We all knew that he was incorruptibly honourable. But he lived in a dilapidated brick villa that was mortgaged up to the chimneys. A stone's throw from him lived a member of parliament who grew richer and richer day by day. Wasn't that enough to prove that there was nothing specially remarkable about being either President or incorruptibly honourable?

Moreover the President had been kidnapped and driven in a car to the eastern border.* Of course this was a criminal action, but one could not forget that it had been done by an element in the population guaranteed to be patriotic. And nobody must be able to accuse the inhabitants of Brändö of a lack of patriotism. Consequently, it was only natural that people should maintain a certain reserve vis-à-vis President Ståhlberg.

There were in fact a number of celebrities in the community, but the prevailing feeling of self-satisfaction acted like a grindstone, the argument being: since he lives here with us he can't be so remarkable. This had nothing to do with modesty, it was merely an expression of the Brändöites' belief that they represented an élite.

An élite who, purely from an instinct of self-preservation, repudiated the thought that membership of Brändö Yachting Club might have demanded any extraordinary spiritual or moral qualities.

This should really have suited Father well. He had not made use of the intellectual gifts he had inherited, and he was demoralized by this betrayal of his own abilities. Unfortunately demoralization never leads to a fixed lower level, but always to something under any predetermined level, that is what is demoralizing. Father mustered up a splendid disdain for the stupidity that surrounded him, which was reflected in his deep self-disgust. It was not surprising that he drank too much.

* In 1930 President Ståhlberg was forced into a car and taken to the Russo-Finnish frontier by a group of right-wing extremists protesting against the spread of communism in Finland.

47

9

It is certain that Father drank a good deal even in his youth. It was in keeping with his highly strung temperament. He aimed his champagne corks at life itself, just as he aimed his shotgun at the clay pigeons. And the more the splinters flew the happier he was. He was like a Greek who loved smashing pottery, or a Russian throwing his empty glass at the wall.

He probably saw himself as some sort of hereditary prince. He was the only child of a highly esteemed cultural personality, related to every well-bred Finn, those who mattered at any rate.

He lived in an age when the ties of kinship still resembled a hammock in which one could safely rest. It was a time when the peoples of the world had not yet crashed together like the billiard-balls on the green baize at the Stock Exchange Club. In his world the laws were much more lenient than they had been in the days of my hard-working maternal grandparents, and more lenient still than they were for those who only had the right to toil from morning to night, though that did not mean that they had the right to work.

He was able to look at life through a champagne glass, and he saw clearly that it was golden, that it bubbled and was fun.

In each bubble a hope rose to the surface. He would become a great baritone singer, but was he good enough? Pop! Best not to find out. Perhaps he could become an incomparable architect? Pop! That would mean such a lot of work that he would have no time to live. He would become the world's happiest being, but he couldn't do that alone. Pop! She had gone off with his handsome, wealthy friend. He would at any rate become rich, as rich as that multi-millionaire Jürgens, whose guest he had been for twenty-four hours at the world championships in marksmanship. Everyone respected money, everyone. Pop! But money respected no one. After the war paper-boys in Berlin had become multi-millionaires like Jürgens. And a gentleman, a real one that is, could lose all he possessed in less time than it took him to knock the ash off his cigar.

The bubbles were born on the bottom of the glass, floated playfully upwards, burst, and were gone.

When Father woke up the next morning his mouth was dry and his hands shaking. He was neither famous, nor rich, nor happy. In the bed beside him lay a woman who would certainly not be unfaithful to him. The thought filled him with disgust. He could only accept passionate faithfulness. Middle-class faithfulness was a sort of deceit because it indicated lack of imagination and submission. Faithfulness to him was not a thing to possess but to win back, or to be won back.

When she woke she would reproach him for having drunk too much. He therefore hurried to the clothes-closet on the upper floor where he had a bottle hidden. He drank half of it and his old self-confidence returned. All that was necessary was a master-shot, a master-stroke worthy of a master marksman and a champion billiard player, that was to say himself, sitting there in the clothes-closet, but who would soon step out into the morning sunshine.

He returned to the bedroom through the twins' room. A well-known odour halted him. His good humour changed instantly to rage.

That damned child had wet the bed again.

49

Father tore him from his bed and flung the wet sheet on the floor where the yellow patch gleamed in a ray of sunlight from the window. Without a word he threw himself on the boy and belaboured his body with clenched fists. The boy moaned, but did not resist.

The other twin jumped from his bed in alarm, took a step backwards, and was unlucky enough to put his foot into the pot which overturned spilling over the striped rag-rug the same liquid that had stained the sheet.

'Idiot!' screamed his father and boxed his ears before slamming the door as he left the room.

That day was ruined.

If his wife had thought of going in to comfort the twins he would have believed she was accusing him. Had he not the right to bring up his own children? Everyone took sides against him. Why must the boys oblige him to use violence which was so repugnant to him? He was the person who needed comfort, he was far too sensitive to live with cretins.

She told him that it was not the boys' fault that he drank. She said that if he cared in the least for his children he would give up drinking.

He said that he did not care in the least for his children. When he said this he admired his own cruelty, but then tears came into his eyes as he reflectd that this was perhaps just what she believed. No one could see any good in him. That was why he drank.

In short, a man whom nobody in the world loved had nothing left but to drink.

She said that everyone loved him. The twins too. It was too easy to love him, therefore he had to make it difficult. She begged him not to make it impossible.

He went in to the boys and gave them some money and told them to buy lemonade. On his way he visited the clothes-closet, and emptied the bottle.

But he still wasn't entirely satisfied.

The boys had not looked happy. There was fear in their eyes. He could not endure anyone being frightened of him when he did not intend it. They ought to be able to appreciate his generosity. They ought to have realized that deep down he was good, but that he was impetuous. That was his nature.

But how could they understand lacking in intelligence as they were? They could not even get on at school. One of them was stuck in the bottom class of the preparatory school. He was ashamed of having such children.

His wife tried to explain to him that the boys might have been injured at birth when their mother died. Perhaps they had been without oxygen at some decisive moment. It was bad enough, anyway, to lose your mother, the noise of whose stomach you had grown accustomed to during the nine months inside her, and which every child heard again in its mother's arms. It was the soothing voice which told you that everything would be all right. Then, suddenly, all that was familiar was cut short, and all the sounds were strange and frightening. Things like that arrest development.

What they needed was love, his love.

He told her that she meant they needed play-acting. He was to pretend to them that he loved them, that was what she meant. Just as she pretended to him that she loved him. But he wasn't going to be taken in, that was why he drank. His children might not be geniuses, but they were not stupid enough to be taken in by false feelings. He was not prepared to degrade himself and his children by acting dishonourably in front of them.

She asked if he truly did not love them.

He then burst into tears and she had to take his head in her arms to comfort him. He pressed his head against her breast, and listened to the sound of her heart. And though he was pretty drunk he managed a sufficient erection to make intercourse possible, after which he slept, calmed for the moment.

The boys had been sitting on their beds listening to the agitated voices in their father's room. They were afraid when their parents quarrelled. They were afraid she would depart like the previous mummy. Then things would be even worse.

She did not, though things got worse all the time. When the boys got bigger and stronger he gave up hitting them. Then they lost the only physical contact they had ever had with their father.

IO

There are two remarks in particular, the twins made in my childhood, neither of which I can ever forget.

The first of these came when I was five, when one of them pointed out that he was twice as old as I was.

I remember that I sat on the wood-box in my paternal grandmother's kitchen and considered the matter. I told him that he would not always be that much older. He said that nothing would change, that he would always be as much older as he was today, and he was twice as old as I was, wasn't he?

'So when I am ten you will be twenty?' I said.

He nodded, 'that's right'.

'And when I am fifty you will be a hundred?' I said.

'No!' he replied, 'for then I shall be dead. No one lives to be a hundred.'

I could not budge him, and the absurdity of the argument scared me. But what scared me most of all was that I was unable to make him see how wrong his calculations were.

He seemed to be implying that while I could never reach fifty he was free to be seventy, eighty, ninety, so long as I was content to be half as old.

The other remark was possibly even more alarming though it too, improbable as it seems, was thoughtless.

I was at the front with the other twin. It was the last year of the war and our optimism had ebbed. Though I was in a trench a hundred metres from the enemy I was still not much more than a child. I was not yet nineteen, not yet an adult at any rate.

My brother was a second lieutenant and in command of the base. He was very daring and looked dashing. A long row of decorations for bravery in the field shone on his chest. He had already been in the army for three years and had been wounded three times, but had constantly asked to return to the front line. He had plenty of experience of war.

I had not.

After a minor intermezzo with fairly intensive artillery fire and a half-hearted attack which we had repulsed, he looked reflectively at me, slapped the leg of his boot with his riding whip (he was really a cavalry officer) and said gloomily: 'Do you know what? This is such a hellish place that we can't possibly both get out of it alive.'

Then his natural optimism got the upper hand and he added: 'But I shan't be the one to fall.'

As I write this I alone am left. All the people who lived on Brändö in my childhood home when I was five are gone. I have not mentioned any of them by name, and I don't intend to do so. They have no names for me, they simply are. They parted with their names to dark, silent stones. I speak of Mother and Father, which would have sounded affected when they were alive, but suit them well now that I have assigned them roles that outlive them.* The twins are the one and the other, and the idea that you may confuse them with one another does not worry me at all. Each had exactly the same start in life, and the way in which a merciless world thought it best to share out misfortunes between them matters less than what they did.

As for my eldest brother his story is so short that the little I have to tell of him does not require me to men-

* A Swedish-speaking child calls its parents *Pappa* and *Mamma*.

tion him by name. It is also worth noting that while he was alive I never heard him called by his proper name. Today there is hardly anyone who even remembers what it was.

Our dog was called Inna.

It was an English setter, black and white and gentle. Father had not bought it for the children, but as a gun dog. It was trained to point sitting birds. When it stopped with one foot in the air and stood dead still staring at a tree or a bush, Father raised his gun and a shot rang out. The bird fell from its perch. The dog had done its job.

If it rushed up to the dead bird Father beat it immoderately. It must only do what it had been taught to do, anything else would bring shame on its owner.

The dog was not a comrade, it was a tool. It was neither he nor she, it was it. Father thought sentimentality ruined a dog. Hitting a dog had nothing to do with your feelings. He hit children too, didn't he?

His violence and intolerance were sometimes so great that I was surprised that he did not attack his car when it refused to start. But it never got so much as a scratch from him, our beautiful, incomparable Reo Flying Cloud, the like of which was never manufactured again.

The car had a back seat with a bench on which Inna sat, her ears flapping in the wind. When times were at their best Father had everything. Car, dog, guns with silver mountings, and a beautiful wife beside him in the front seat when he drove out to his friend's estate to shoot.

He brought down a great deal of game there, and — alas, alas — his friend brought down his wife.

Inna remained in the house longer than my mother, Inna was faithful.

Often enough Inna took the place of my mother for me. When my parents were away all night and wolves breathed behind the curtains Inna and I slept on the hall mat by the front door. My head rested on the dog's furry coat, and when Mother and Father at last returned it lay motionless, gently wagging its tail in order not to wake the sleeping child.

I loved that dog so deeply that I ought to love all dogs, but I don't. I really detest them. I can't stand their servility. I can be just as impatient as my father was, when they don't understand what I want of them.

But Inna was not a dog at all to me. Inna was security and love. Everything has the wrong labels, and when you talk about your dog you are expressing a longing for your mother. That is why names are so utterly unnecessary.

One day when Inna was more than ten years old the twins came running home to say that Inna was lying dead in the forest. Father went with them to the glade where the dog lay. He softly called its name and the dog struggled to its feet, took a few steps, whined a little, and fell dead at his feet. Inna displayed a dog's most human characteristic: faithfulness unto death to its oppressor.

I was in town with my maternal grandparents when news of Inna's death reached me. I took my bicycle and, crying bitterly, rode about the streets for hours so that no one should see how much I mourned a dog.

I have many pictures of my mother. So many that together they could illustrate everything that I can imagine
a woman might be and do. They are photos, mind-
pictures, fantasy-pictures.

I never drew her. It was plain to me that I should
never succeed in capturing her image, she simply had
no image for me.

But there is a photo that my father took of her when
they were newly married. She is sitting on a sofa looking
very soulful. She wears a strange serpent-like necklace
which hangs down over her breast (the little that was
allowed in the Twenties). Her arms are bare, and one
hand is resting in the other. She has a long, beautiful
neck. Her eyes are cloudy, she is very lovely. My father
had a good box-camera with a cloth under which he
put his head. The subject had to sit still for a long time.
Mother must have had to look soulful for several minutes.

I should like to be able to say that I had a soulful
mother.

But Mother herself told me that she looked odd in that
photo because she wasn't quite sober, not an unusual
state for her at that time. She and Father wanted life to
be festive, and they thought the best way to make it so
was to rush from party to party. They kept it up until
the parties turned into monotonous repetitions that bored
them, and the smiles on their faces stiffened to ice.

These were only thawed by kisses in dark corridors,
behind the lilac bushes, in the pantry, on the way up-

stairs, in the bedroom. When the other did not see, but suspected.

The time between the parties was used up by accusations, evasions, lies and confessions. They confused drunken quarrels with passion, and they exploited each other, simultaneously growing estranged. When they were finally divorced they were like two lifeboats drifting out of sight of one another on the wide sea into which their brightly-lit luxury yacht had sunk, after striking an iceberg which should only have been supplying them with ice for the champagne coolers.

The catastrophe left no visible external marks. Mother was as beautiful as ever, in fact she was perhaps more desirable than formerly. I saw no more of her than before. She gave me a hug and a kiss in passing, and this was clearly precisely what a boy of about ten needed to make him mad about his mother. She knew how to handle men.

Or did she?

There was no lack of them about her. She slipped out of a marriage suitable to her station into a trinity ruled by beauty, good taste, and riches, chiefly by riches.

The person who sat on the biggest mound of money was Maire Gullichsen, and round her mound danced my mother, in the company of sundry idlers and geniuses. The circle had a distinctly artistic and intellectual character. It was made up of painters, critics, architects and designers, and the foundation of Artek* was one result of their activities. Artek was made world famous by Alvar Aalto's ingenious method of bending veneers and piling stools on top of one another.

Mother's only contribution to this enterprise was her self-sacrificing attempt to cure the chronic impotence of one of its devotees. She cannot have succeeded for when

* A famous firm of furniture makers in Helsinki.

58

the war came he rushed towards a machine-gun and was killed. It was said that he did so because he could not make a real stand, a joke as tasteless as it is inappropriate when you are talking of a dead hero.

Another member of the group was said to have preferred a hero's death to the spiritual impotence as an artist that had befallen him when he married money, and was compelled by his father-in-law to design sweet-papers. But this is probably not true. His mistress was a showgirl from Paris, and she was as delicious and black as a stick of liquorice. She performed without wrapping and the man who chose a bullet instead of her must really have been out of his mind.

Indeed they tried with a combination of wit and sentimentality to keep reality at arm's length. They tried with might and main to prevent time from carrying off beauty, and the Bolsheviks from taking their money. Their success was partial.

But everything happened slowly, imperceptibly, it was only through me that my mother could see that she was getting older. I entered my teens and began to understand enough to be a nuisance. This does not mean that I had any moral prejudices, but her own emancipation was so superficial that her child gave her a bad conscience. It wasn't necessary to scrape away much of her make-up to expose the petit-bourgeois mentality she had picked up in Lahti, the town of her school-days. Then she would take a drink and become soulful and remote and I could not reach her. That was what drove me to despair.

She too was now living with my maternal grandparents, her parents. She and I shared a room, which may have accorded with the laws of nature, but not with common sense. You see, she frequently came home in the early morning, if in fact she came home at all. And if she came she hardly ever did so without waking me. Things had a habit of getting in her way as she fumbled noisily about in the dark. By degrees I did not dare to go to sleep, but sat at the dining-room window, staring out all night at the empty street, waiting for her to come. To see how well her legs were carrying her, and whether it would be necessary to try to keep clattering objects out of her way, so that Grandmother would not be woken up.

My placid, sensible grandmother could not endure her daughter's drunkenness. She burst out with angry threats and warnings. I threw myself between them and howled that Mummy was ill, my mummy was ill, ill, ill. . . .

I picked up a paper-knife and threatened my grandmother, and then she fell silent and did not utter another word, and that was worse.

She *was* ill too, my mother. And day by day she grew worse, her will became as flabby as her skin. She promised her son penance and that she would turn over a new leaf. She gave these promises as an impatient mother gives her child sweets, so that it will stop pestering her.

But she never kept a single promise. I found it more and more difficult to love her, but I did my best. I did not want to let her down as my father had done.

My perpetual nightly vigils made me tired and wan, and nervous tension and anxiety made it difficult for me to concentrate at school. I was not a good pupil, and only managed to rise from class to class by the skin of my teeth.

Mother persuaded herself that I had a mother-fixation and tried to divert my interest in her goings-on by paying for riding lessons for me at the riding-school across the street.

She spoke so enthusiastically about riding that I got it into my head that she wanted me to become a good horseman. I was quite small when I began and the horses were very large, and I was frightened of them. I have never shaken off this apprehension and a closer acquaintanceship with horses has shown me how justified it is.

All the same I climbed boldly on to the saddle and tried to imagine to myself that I liked riding. I remember with special annoyance what my behind felt like when our merciless riding master ordered a quick trot. I often got landed with a gigantic elderly Hannoverian who must have come to the country with von der Goltz to relieve Mannerheim. This wooden old object's trot jolted me so terribly that I thought my poor private parts would be annihilated. How the cavalry men had anything to give the ladies after their daily exercises was a riddle to me.

But as usual everything is the opposite of what we believe. As we all know cavalry men are incomparable bucks whom no woman can resist. That is why they have red breeches so that you can see immediately where they keep their stoutest weapon. And I cannot deny that even at that time I coveted both their red breeches and a future as a lady-killer. That was what we boys dreamed of when we sat together and tossed off in an empty horse-box that smelt of hay and horse-piss.

I overcame my fear and actually became a good horseman. I won one silver goblet after another and reached the climax of my equestrian career when I won the Sisu trophy on the horse Camilla. She really belonged to my father's former brother-in-law. He had once been a bank director, and had invested Father's money so badly that we never saw a trace of it again. His spell in prison gave him a chance to ponder his activities.

He was an agreeable man and a real gentleman, and though he had ruined a lot of people no one believed that he had done so intentionally. The fact that he could still afford to keep a saddle-horse after he came out of prison simply proved that he was a real gentleman. He also lived as a respected citizen until the day his horse threw him and broke his neck. People said, with the greatest respect, that it was undoubtedly the death he would have wished if he had been able to choose.

I received the Sisu trophy from the hands of General Hugo Österman, who commanded our defence forces. In the military atmosphere in which we lived, I felt my prize had been handed to me by a being comparable only to the archangels who stood beside our Lord. Later on, I had time to change my opinion of generals, though I still felt a pang of disappointment when, after what had been for him an unusually unfortunate war, I saw him coming towards me in the street, degraded now to an insurance agent. In some way it took away the lustre of my prize, and I no longer bothered to polish it.

The step from the riding-school to the volunteer defence corps was not a big one. I enlisted in a cavalry division and by doing so ruined my Sunday morning rests with drills and weapon practice. I could no longer manage to sit up night after night waiting for my mother.

I changed slowly but surely into a strong, healthy young man, on whom my country could count in her hour of danger, which, indeed, she was working towards.

Mother watched my development with satisfaction. She was planning a future for me as a captain of horse or a gynaecologist. She said that I was good-looking and well-built and that I should be perfectly suited to either profession. It all depended on which end I liked best, the head or the tail. She considered that she need no longer worry about my future, and she intensified her efforts to ruin her own.

I was not a good pupil at school, but I always got a high mark for church history.

This is rather strange as I never got hold of the text book on church history, still less did I pay any attention in lessons. You might suppose that my success was due to my ancestor the archbishop, but it wasn't that at all. Bishop Jacob Tengström was a rotten traitor who made peace with the Russians in 1809, even though they had not advanced beyond Österbotten.*

Moreover, ancestors had no influence on our marks at the Old Finnish Co-education School.† Only at the entrance examination were they a help. The school was chock full of the children of famous people. They were so much in the majority that you could claim that some sort of equality prevailed. Descendants of Sibelius were there, and almost every class contained an offspring of E. E. Sillanpää, the author and Nobel Prizewinner. There was a count whose ancestor had been Governor General of Finland, and the children and grandchildren of presidents and ministers, children of generals, of leaders of industry, and wealthy people in general. In short, it was

* Tikkanen is being sarcastic. The Russians advanced into Sweden beyond the Swedish border town of Torneå at the northernmost tip of the Gulf of Bothnia, and the whole of Finland was occupied. Tengström represented church interests at the Diet that negotiated with the Russians in 1809.
† The school in which Finnish was the first language. Many Swedish-speaking families sent their children to it realizing that it would be an advantage to know Finnish.

here that preparations were being made for the next usurping of power by the twenty Swedish-speaking families who owned Finland. To some extent it succeeded for those twenty families are now bilingual.

My good marks in church history were due to the fact that my teacher in the subject, Lauri Pohjanpää, could see into the future. He let me draw during his lessons without disturbing me, but when the lesson was over he came to my desk and gathered up my drawings, saying that he would keep them and grow rich when I became a famous artist.

I was pleased that he let me draw instead of stuffing me with the dates of stupid ecclesiastical gatherings, but I wondered if he knew that he was really talking to a future gynaecologist, with captain of horse in reserve.

But his conviction was unshakable and I still ask myself whether this was because he was a clergyman, or owing to the fact that he was a good poet – with the reputation of having once had an exciting relationship with a ballet-dancer.

He never failed to give me an eight on my report, and this raised my average enough, to let me scrape into the next class. My five for drawing was poor support for his prophecy, but the ways of art are inscrutable for the old fellow was right. He never did grow rich on my drawings but, in a better world, I hope he is pleased that the only poem I know by heart is one that he wrote. It tells of a hare who feared he might be shot in the forest. The poem appealed to me for, unlike my comrades, I did not regard dying in the bloom of youth, clothed in an SS uniform, as my highest ambition.

Yet it was the hare in my make-up that caused me to enlist as a volunteer for the front. I could not bear living with the suspicion that I might be more cowardly than others, and I had to put myself to the test before the war ended. As things turned out it did not end all

64

that quickly, and I had time to acquire a pretty good idea of what it was like to be a hare.

I cannot remember that anyone expected me to become an artist. At any rate no one pushed the idea. I believe that though they certainly thought art was a civilizing influence, they did not think the people who practised it were civilized.

Among my mother's followers, however, there was one who unconsciously affected my future. He was a wealthy Jew who dealt in furs. He gave Mother a book entitled *Die zeitlose Kunst*. It contained a selection of works of art made by another Jew and based exclusively on his personal choice. This selection made an unforgettable impression on me because of the synthesis of art that it gave.

This happened at much the same time that Adolf Hitler began to burn works of art he did not like, to be followed later by the burning of Jews or anyone else whose taste differed from his. It became apparent that art was not just wall decoration, but something that expressed life's deepest meaning. Works of art were bunkers in the front line of the defence of freedom and man's integrity.

I suspected this but did not yet understand why. No one told me it was so either. Most people thought that Jews did not understand art, and agreed that they were possibly both Wall Street's lackeys and agents of the Soviet secret service. The furrier left the country to save his own skin.

The advantage of wealth is that it gives the wealthy the chance to escape from war and misery. But often enough they do not need to flee, as war seldom threatens wealth. People are killed and frontiers are changed but in general the rich remain rich. They belong to a class which has succeeded in keeping itself above the futilities of war. On the other hand revolutions threaten the rich and this explains their eagerness to support the defence forces. These are the best guarantee for maintaining the established order, even if careless sabre rattling can lead to war, which results in falls on the stock market and trade depressions. But business men are obliged to take risks.

Another good thing about wealth is that it promotes culture. When a certain degree of affluence is reached the wealthy person is irresistibly driven towards some activity that benefits culture. This usually happens in the generation that has ceased to belch at table and no longer boasts about its wealth. People then become patrons of art, if not for reasons connected with the technicalities of taxation, then from sheer boredom.

My maternal grandmother's sister, Vera, who gave me a book about Holbein, was already cultured when she became rich. She grew rich by marrying a brewer who died shortly after the wedding. Holbein portrayed Henry VIII and his wives, who were not as lucky in love as my grandmother's sister, which was perhaps why she chose that particular book. In any case Holbein's drawings made me realize that to grow to be a good artist is more important than the models you portray.

A lead pencil was the way to eternal life, and I am grateful to kind Vera for that discovery. It was more valuable to me than inheriting her whole brewery would have been.

For a time this loomed on the horizon as a possibility, for she lived as a widow for many years and someone had to inherit the business. I had frequently taken her fox-terrier, Pusi, out for runs, so I stood a chance.

But as the years passed Pusi grew blind and bumped into chairs and tables and I wouldn't go out with it any longer. To put it bluntly I thought the animal should be put down and its misery brought to an end, but Vera had not the heart to have that done. Then a Colonel appeared on the scene and offered to exercise her blind dog. By way of thanks she married him. She died shortly afterwards and away went my inheritance.

In the book which I had received from Grandmother's sister Vera, there was a picture of Erasmus of Rotterdam and I drew comfort from his words. He says that 'business men are the basest and vainest of people. They engage in the most rotten and most degrading occupation you can imagine, and they engage in it in the most disgraceful way, by lying, bearing false witness, stealing, cheating and continually trying to deceive their fellow men. All the same they elbow their way to the front everywhere, and want to be first because their fists are full of gold.'

I could therefore count myself lucky that I was not obliged to foist bad beer on people while swelling up with self-conceit myself.

Unfortunately I did not remember Erasmus's words about Bacchus, 'that he liberates man from his sorrows and anxieties, but this liberation only lasts for a short time. When the intoxication is over anxiety returns – and now at full gallop.'

One night, when I had waited in vain for my mother to come home from the pub, I had promised on my bare knees never to touch a drop of liquor. In spite of this I did, and in my folly helped to increase the poor Colonel's fortune (and thereby his absurdity). Something he, like the old soldier he was, bore with his accustomed fortitude.

My share of the inheritance was the gruesome hangover that comes from drinking beer.

Of course neither my mother, nor my mother's parents in Norra Järnvägsgatan, nor my father on Brändö were prepared to subject themselves to a proletarian dictatorship, and they never questioned the wisdom of the measures our political leaders were taking. Once the Winter War had started we threw ourselves into it heart and soul.

The war did my mother nothing but good. She became active and happy now that she no longer had time to make trouble for herself with muddled love-affairs. She considerably reduced her consumption of drink and aspirins. When paratroopers were hunted out in our dark cellar she showed a courage that amazed everyone. And for the first time for many years she overcame her dislike of the Minister's bad breath. When he came to visit her with a box of chocolates under his arm, she kissed him on the mouth to show that he had her full support. This healthy life rejuvenated her and she became beautiful and attractive again. But the Minister, who was weighed down by a heavy load of responsibility for his country's welfare, was not able to rejoice over the blessings that the war had brought him. He no longer suggested that they flee to Monte Carlo, but with heavy footsteps shuffled off to the Parliament House. He knew how black things looked now that the Germans and the Russians had carved up Poland between them, and the Allies were only able to send limited supplies of moral support.

The first bombs on the city fell just round our house. All the windows were blown in and my mother's sister, who was expecting a child, was thrown against a wall, and my grandmother's youngest sister was knocked over and received a shock that brought on Parkinson's disease. After that she trembled for the rest of her life as if she lived in constant fear.

My grandmother would have been on the exact spot where the nearest bomb exploded had she not remembered just before that she had forgotten to buy buns and turned off into Helminen's bakery.

So there is good reason to say that the communists wasted no time in showing their dislike for my family. On that first day I rushed straight from school to the headquarters of the defence corps, where we shot at the bombers from the courtyard with ordinary army rifles. We did not hit a single plane – better still we did not hit one another.

Father put on his Olympic marksman's uniform and, with his best rifle over his shoulder, made his way to the strong point at Brändö bridge. There, standing on a rock by the shore, he prepared to shoot down the first bomber to come within range. None of them did that day, nor did he have better luck on any of the three succeeding days, so he tired of the war and went back to quarrelling with his wife. The ennobling effects of the war on him were minimal.

The fact that Brändö, like Switzerland, was never subjected to a real bombing attack in the Second World War gradually made him feel like the citizen of a neutral state, though of course he had his preferences and antipathies. He aired these at the Stock Exchange Club to which he betook himself daily, defying death by crossing a narrow wooden bridge, and passing two petrol-tanks and a gasworks. Sometimes he was in such a poor shape when he came home that, like the gallant von Essen in *The Tales of Ensign Stål*, he had to be carried upstairs.

To his sons, who knew nothing of the intrigues of the Comintern, this was more distressing than the war itself.

Little by little they had given up hope that their father would ever pull himself together, and try to live a life that he and others could put up with. He had always been a dominant personality, and when he was happy his whole environment was infected by his happiness. When he was distressed everyone was distressed. When he felt miserable we all felt miserable.

It is easy to pick him out as the person to blame for the calamity that befell his eldest son. Even though, in the circumstances, many other culprits could have been found, and as many other reasons as you please. Owing to my brother's self-control and his reserved nature we shall never know the reason for his desperate deed. He never said a word about what weighed him down.

It might have been the war, of course. War summons man to death. War is man's way of demonstrating the impossibility of life.

But the purpose of war is not to die or to turn the other cheek, but to kill. Father had taught us boys to shoot, but he had never urged us to shoot at others. On the contrary, he never failed to impress on us the responsibility of having a gun.

Can it be said that on this point he displayed a lack of patriotic spirit?

Unfortunately the power of example is greater than the power of the word, and Father was not always a good example, indeed he was seldom a good example. Every time he became depressed, which happened unfailingly whenever he was drunk, he waved a gun and threatened to commit suicide. It is true that he never did so. At the last minute he always decided that he would read the *History of Rome*, or Chledowskis's *The Court at Ferrara* just once more before he ended his life. So he was saved by his thirst for culture, but it did not save his sons. The thought of suicide was imprinted on our minds. He had shown us a secret door and taken away the placard saying 'danger'.

Indeed, it is very easy to pick him out as the culprit. He probably thought of himself as such.

Even so, it is conceivable that in this case it was self-sacrificing love not negligent egotism that was to blame. It is possible that the culprit lived downstairs among the palms and marble statuettes by Valter Runeberg. Anyway it was to my father's mother that the angel came after it had happened.

My eldest brother, who was twenty-one when the war started, was immediately called up and sent to a training centre in Österbotten. A civilian, you see, is altogether too tame to be sent to the front. My brother like all the rest had to undergo a short course in obedience and fury. When you have learned to hate and to obey your officers you are also fit to be killed. The procedure suits most people, our army is incomparable, but regrettable exceptions do occur.

My brother loved butterflies and quiet piano music. He would sit alone in the darkest corner of the room and play his flute. His father's mother met his wishes even before he had had time to express them. She filled him with her own anxieties about the dangers of life, but he shut them away, he never let his fear out.

My father's mother had not prepared her son for the demands life makes on a human being, and for that he could reproach her. She had definitely not prepared her grandson for the demands a war makes, but for that no one can reproach her. Yet this may have been the very reason why things turned out as they did.

On his first leave from the training centre he was in

71

a black mood and confided to his father that he was nervous. Father did not find this difficult to understand. The communiqués from the front certainly told of incredibly glorious victories, but the price of these victories was not small. Who was not afraid of dying, or had not at least the right to feel a bit nervous? Why, you even felt tense before a competition in marksmanship.

That is what Father said. He mentioned the world championships in Berlin.

My brother smiled quietly and said that wasn't the trouble.

Father asked him what it was.

My brother said he didn't know, he wanted to see a doctor. He said all this very calmly.

Father then made an appointment for him to see his own psychiatrist. My brother went to see him in uniform. In contrast to his brothers he was not tall and well-built, he was squat and looked dejected, a pretty miserable sort of soldier. He complained to the doctor about his bad nerves, said he couldn't stand it. He said it all very calmly.

The doctor said there was nothing the matter with him. The doctor patted him on the shoulder and said that everything was fine. Finally the doctor said that the country needed all her sons, particularly those who were good shots.

These words pleased Father. He interpreted them as a personal compliment. At the dinner-table he informed us all that he intended to enlist for the front as a sniper. He wanted to be with his sons. But he had to swallow one word, he had nearly said that he wanted to die with his sons.

Only one son was at the front. This was the twin Father had beaten for wetting his bed. When the war began he had nearly completed his military service as a volunteer in Nyland's dragoons, into which, beguiled by my interest in riding, he had asked to enlist. He had stopped wetting his bed in the very first week. He and another bed-wetter had been put by turns in the upper and lower bunks, and after a few nights both were dry. There were great psychologists in the army who knew how to make men out of boys.

Three sons were sitting at the table and one of them couldn't swallow his food. Father thought this was the right moment to open a bottle of red wine, for he wanted to celebrate his brave decision. We all knew that by so doing he had postponed putting it into action for at least a fortnight. Meanwhile he would be well on the way to killing himself again, and his wife would be obliged to call the doctor, who would come bounding along with his syringes. There was no mistake about Father's bad nerves, for they were really bad and needed both the doctor and his medicines.

After dinner I went down to Grandmother's flat with my eldest brother, partly to escape the quarrel that had already started, and partly because I had an indefinable feeling that I ought not to leave the depressed soldier on his own. What could I say to him? He was almost seven years older than I was, and he already knew everything. He even knew that something bad was going to happen, he told me so.

I asked him what that was and to whom it would happen.

He looked at me strangely and said that bad things happen to everyone. If they didn't then they were not bad.

I grew frightened and did not dare to ask any more questions. It was as if the questions might have led us straight to the horror itself. I asked him to play his flute.

He sat on his bed, put the flute to his lips, and began to blow. The tune was the one about the three little pigs.

73

The first built his house of straw and the second of twigs, and the wicked wolf came and blew them down. But before he came to the end where the wolf tries in vain to blow down the third little pig's house of stone he had stopped blowing. The flute had sunk onto his lap and he was staring right through me without seeing anything.

I asked him if he was ill, if I should call a doctor.

Then he laughed and said he was quite well, the doctor had already told him so, and that he was going back to his camp by the evening train. I felt relieved and, helped by his laugh, I slunk away with a hesitant good-bye.

I did not dare to touch him. If I had hugged him he would have thought I was a drip.

After I left him he went to Grandmother and asked for a couple of strong sleeping-tablets. She gave them to him, maybe she thought he wanted to sleep on the train. He took the pills and went to his room. Half an hour later Grandmother heard a shot. When she went to his room he was lying on his bed with the death-rattle in his throat. He had shot himself in the temple with a nine millimetre parabellum.

On the upper floor we heard the shot too, and when Father went down to discover what had happened he found his mother dusting in the living-room. She said quite briefly, 'Well, that's that.'

A couple of evenings later the angel visited her. It stood beside her bed and looked at her with an unfathomable expression. She got out of bed and stood beside the angel. They remained like that for a long time, although her legs were bad and grew tired with standing. Then the angel dissolved and was gone.

I asked her what the angel looked like, and she said it looked just like one Valter Runeberg had sculptured, a very nice angel. The angel had come to tell her that all was well. It had not said anything, perhaps because

74

it did not speak Swedish. Finnish-speaking angels were something Grandmother could not imagine. Moreover, angels do not need to say anything for their message is always the same: salvation.

14

The day we buried my brother was as cold and lofty as a Gothic cathedral. And up in its roof where as a rule angels disport themselves, bombers hummed, the angels of war. To be buried in wartime was to be buried at the right time, the time of death.

The only trouble was that my brother had not died in the right way.

Not much is needed to make you a hero. You only need to be killed by a foreigner. You need never meet your slayer, or even see him. It is enough if you are hit.

What had my brother got against foreigners that made him give them the slip? Nothing. He did not know them, anymore than he knew the people who did not live on Brändö. It was due to a flaw in his upbringing that he did not find it natural to hate them, or to scorn those who spoke another language. He even objected to Grandmother's assertion that all Finns were ruffians. Her father, like Mannerheim, had been a high-ranking Russian officer, and there was never any suggestion that the Russians were ruffians. Consequently it was contradictory that we, along with the Finns who were ruffians, should kill Russians who were not ruffians. And his life in a community sheltered from poverty had not taught him that poor people are the real enemies of the well-to-do, whom the latter are obliged to kill, if they don't want to part with their wealth. This was not necessary in a democracy like Finland where those in need show patience and forbearance with the incapacity of the well-to-do to improve their conditions. Besides, the pattern of the war was so complicated that it was not always easy to see that it was a settlement of accounts between the rich and the poor. There were poor people on both sides, the rich had the power to persuade and the means to employ them in their service. You might also find rich people opposing one another, which was confusing, and made you ask whether they were not betraying their class. They were not, it was simply that prevailing conditions had forced them to take surprising measures in the struggle for their common country, which is called Capital.

My brother, who understood nothing of this, had no acceptable motive either for killing or for being killed. Consequently all that remained for him was to take his own life. On the other hand he had no lack of reasons for doing so.

It was a wretchedly small, wretched group of wretched looking people standing by the black hole in the hard frozen ground of the old churchyard. It was his mother's grave, and beside it stood his father, his father's third wife, and his brothers. Between the trees was a glimpse of Lappviken's lunatic asylum, where his paternal great-grandfather had ended his days, after wearing himself out in his struggle for the education and equality of the oppressed majority in his country.

Father was wearing his marksman's uniform which united him with the people in the world who can afford to shoot clay pigeons. He had something white in one corner of his mouth and his gaze was glassy. He was so drunk that instead of being cold he was able to feel a painful pleasure at the insult that had been offered him.

He used to say: 'There are three corners to my hat,

77

if it has not three corners it is not my hat.'* It was obvious that his son did not have three corners, and the grave into which his urn was sunk had four round stones, one in each corner. In the middle was a square stone which the frozen ground had at some time pushed a fraction aslant. On the stone was the name of Father's first wife. I don't think he had visited her grave since her burial, but maybe he began to compare the difference between his wives, the one who lay under the stone and the one beside him.

The dead one directed no criticism at him, while he could feel the living one's disapproval on the nape of his neck. She was standing immediately behind him ready to grab his coat-tail if he gave a lurch. She stood there grey and purposeful, with straggly hair, watchful eyes, and tight-pressed lips, leaning slightly forwards, her legs apart, ready to act instantly. Agitation and constant anxiety had washed away the youthful beauty from her face. She had become a sort of Dorian Gray's portrait to him. The more profligate he became the more it showed in her face. His pact with the devil had protected his outer man. Under his slouch hat he looked just as demonic as he had done in the far off days when he went to brilliant parties with his first wife, and they rode down the stairs at Villa Heiroth on silver trays.

Why couldn't he exchange the living for the dead? Couldn't he get back the smiling woman who had loved him when she left him just as she was giving him the greatest gift a woman can bestow on a man, a child? Yes, two. His eyes filled with tears of self-pity, and he longed to be with her in the black hole.

He pointed to her name on the stone written in gold and said pathetically: 'Do you want more of the same?'

My hatred of him kept my tears at bay, but when I

* An old German folk rhyme.

got home I burst out crying and wept for a long time, though not as long as for our dog. I thought about this and wondered whether I had loved the dog more than my brother, or whether it was that dogs disappear entirely when they die, while human beings leave unanswered questions behind them.

I have never found out why he shot himself.

15

It does not matter which theory of how Finland became embroiled in the war is the right one. What is certain is that the war was necessary. Sensible and far-sighted politicians provided us with it to bring to an end the internal dissensions that had existed since the Civil War. The people were united, and the nation gained the identity which is a necessary condition for lasting independence. Our hundred heroic days corresponded to the hundreds of years of cultural struggle that more fortunately situated peoples pass through. We fought our way to a place in the consciousness of the world.

But though my father's father had sat many times on the steps of our national poet Runeberg's veranda, the spirit of Runeberg no longer reigned in my father's house. My eldest brother had ruined the war for us. Father could not rid himself of his spleen even though one of the twins came home seriously wounded and with a medal.

Moreover, on Christmas-eve there was an air raid warning, and while we were down in the cellar the dog ate the Christmas ham.

And the twin who had been wounded gnashed his teeth as he slept and his brother refused to sleep with him. Sometimes he screamed, waking everyone in the house.

When he was awake he told us time after time how he had got the wound in his buttock, and how he had sat leaning against a birch while the blood ran into the white snow. The temperature was minus forty and the more blood he lost the warmer it seemed to get. Then he slept and when he woke up he was in hospital.

The dream he had leaning against the tree must have been horrid, because now as soon as he fell asleep he had a nightmare. When he was awake he was brave, and said he wanted to return to the front.

The war suited him as well as his cavalry uniform. For the first time in his life he had been rewarded for wetting his pants. It became apparent that he had something that other people lacked: he had courage. He also lacked something that others possessed: imagination. Even though he had already been wounded he could not imagine that he might be killed. If his elder brother had found it too difficult to live, he believed that it was impossible to die if you did not will it yourself. He was a self-made Achilles and therefore had little to fear from the war and everything to gain.

The war compensated him for Father's contempt and scorn. Father realized this and drank even more than usual. Everything seemed to him lamentable, just like a competition where you make a mess of the first shot and then lose interest.

To make everything even more lamentable for him I announced that I was going to the front as a despatch-rider. I think I meant what I said, at any rate I remember feeling like the soldier boy whose father was to be found where the beakers swung thickest.* In his alarm Father sent me to spend the Christmas holidays in the country at a manor-house owned by his wife's relatives. The country looked like a Christmas card and it would have been very boring if there had not been a

* A reference to Johan Ludvig Runeberg's poem *The Soldier Boy*, but in it the boy's father is a hero.

young girl who had a passion for showing me her behind.

She was so young that she had no down on her fork, but the sight was new to me and I must admit that it stimulated me. She did not improve matters by pawing me and finally she tempted me into the sauna where we lay on the cold ledge and rubbed our tummies together. When we came out an enemy plane flew over at a height of some tens of metres and fired a short salvo at the courtyard. I realized that this was God's way of punishing us for the sin we had committed, but the girl, who in spite of her tender years was more developed than I was, said that it certainly was not, for the Russians did not believe in God, and they were not the sort of people He would employ.

On the other hand it may have been God who prevented the bullets from hitting us, he probably thought that a fright was enough. Of course I am not at all sure that God concerns himself with juveniles in wartime, when they so often meet with misfortunes at other times too. He probably left the home-front entirely to itself as He had promised his full support to the crusade our brave boys were carrying on in the East.

This is the only acceptable explanation of why He could allow the accident that ended my maternal grandfather's life. For Grandfather was an honourable man who had always done what he believed to be right, so you could never censure him even if you could argue about what is right and how right it is.

Once, as chairman of the town council of Lahti, he had to listen to an Easter sermon in which the parson droned on endlessly about the road to Emmaus. At last Grandfather lost patience, struck his stick loudly on the floor, rose to his feet and announced: 'Now I, at all events, am going!' upon which he marched out of the church. To have taken offence at such a trifle would

82

have been grudging and mean since such a demonstration was fully justified.

The disciples on their way to Emmaus certainly had plenty of problems, but their journey did not involve keeping a look-out for cars or for railway-crossings. This, however, is just what Grandfather should have done, though he was only going as far as Bocksbacka.

One crackingly cold winter's day he was out on official business in a car. A policeman was driving and when they came to a level-crossing he stopped as one should. Hoar frost had iced up the side windows completely and you could not see out of them. The policeman wound down the window and heard the train coming.

The train thundered past and when it had gone he drove over. When he was half way across another train came from the opposite direction and hit the back of the car where Grandfather was sitting. The policeman was unhurt, but Grandfather was not so lucky. His chest was crushed and he had other internal injuries and haemorrhages as well. In spite of the shock he did not lose consciousness, and when the ambulance arrived he gave orders, in his capacity as chief medical officer of the Nyland military district, that he was to be taken home instead of to hospital. Apart from his official standing Grandfather was not a man you willingly dared to oppose, and though he was half dead, his will was unbroken. He had been with Grandmother ever since they were married, and he intended to be with her to the end.

Only once had Grandmother, not knowing that he had a patient, opened the door of his consulting-room and caught him with a naked woman on his lap. Grandfather himself was wearing a white coat, a waistcoat, a stiff collar and stiff cuffs and, according to his own account, had had nothing to do with the woman's improper

83

behaviour, which had taken him completely by surprise. If Grandmother had not believed him she would never have told me the story. Their marriage was a very happy one.

Indeed, it was so happy that Grandfather used to say that if they had not had their eldest daughter, my mother, they would have been too happy. Of course this was said after Father's senseless and disastrous worship of Mother had ruined the good upbringing Grandmother had given her.

At the time the accident happened I was sitting in the bus on my way home from the manor-house. I was quite suddenly seized by an inexplicable anxiety which lasted for some time. It was not like ordinary car sickness, and I could not think what was the matter with me. But when I got back to town Grandfather, already terribly weak, lay in his bed and I found out that the accident had happened at the very time that I had felt so uneasy. Something had given the bonds between us a violent wrench, and now everything was hanging on a slender thread. Grandfather was dying and I felt that he was my real father and Grandmother my real mother. Without them I should have been as lost as my brothers. I was deeply shaken.

And Grandfather was not only a father to me, he was also the hero in my life. He was fearless, just, and the comrade who never let me down. However sleepy I was at three o'clock in the morning he always took me with him on his fishing trips, and I was allowed to row both to and from the reef where we fished.

Now I had to watch him fighting off death for more than a week, without hope or penicillin. Not by a look or a quaver in his voice did he reveal any fear.

He must have been in terrible pain for his broken ribs had penetrated his lungs. Nevertheless, he sat up in bed, supported by pillows, and gave orders to his assistant whom he had summoned to his bedside. He kept this up even to the last day, and in my eyes he too became a war hero.

Professor Bardy looked after him. The professor, who was not much younger than Grandfather, visited his patients on a bicycle, wearing a coquettish feather in his Tyrolean hat and golfing plus-fours. He had a new, young wife, and a new youth, and his conversation with Grandfather was heartily coarse.

One day when he entered the sick-room he sniffed audibly and burst out: 'God, what a stink!'

'Gangrene,' said Grandfather.

'You're right. So that's that,' said the professor.

For the second time in this war I heard those fateful words that meant dead and done for.

'This evening?' said Grandfather.

The professor nodded.

Then Grandfather smiled.

'You won't be long behind me, young girls soon kill off conceited old men,' he said.

'We'll see about that,' said the professor cockily. But Grandfather was right, and right too in his assumption that death would be the next visitor that day.

Late that evening he called his whole family to him and we all stood round his bed except Grandmother, who sat on the edge of the bed and stroked his forehead. He looked at us in turn, calmly and without haste, as if preferring to estimate each one's chance in life rather than say good-bye. He seemed to be pleased with what he saw for when he had done he nodded to us all and closed his eyes for the last time.

I did not notice when he ceased to breathe and we were not sure until Grandmother held a mirror to his mouth and the glass remained clear. The mists of life no longer blurred Grandfather's image. Nothing could be added, and nothing taken from him.

16

The load of our heavy peace was made less burdensome by hectic preparations for a new war. We marched and drilled in the defence corps, and at school we were pumped full of patriotism. The World War rumbled on like a distant thunder-cloud on the other side of the gulf. Hitler scored victory after victory.

From the other side of the gulf came one troopship after another carrying German soldiers who were landed at Uleåborg. Across the gulf too came cargoes of weapons, so that we were soon better armed than before the Winter War.

Hopes were high and the Russian spies must have been struck blind since they did not seem to notice what we were up to. It is true that they had a non-aggression pact with Germany, but they could hardly have believed that hundreds of thousands of German soldiers were holiday-making in Lapland while the war was at its height. Nor that we intended to drive the Germans out with the arms we were buying from them.

Perhaps war was like the road accidents that had deprived me of both my grandfathers. There was nothing to be done about it, you had to let it take its course. Besides, to try to prevent a country from going to war was to encroach upon its sovereignty, though for it to attack and destroy another country was quite in order. Finland was still a sovereign country, and to prove this to the world we were preparing for war.

It would also have been stupid not to take part in a

victorious war and we had no intention of being stupid. From a military point of view we chose well, winning most of the battles except a few in the final stages.

All this warlike activity meant that my school-work suffered and I was left behind in the seventh form. But again I was lucky, for among my new class-mates was a pretty girl with whom I fell in love. Or rather I did not. As I, like my father, was a tragic person, incapable of loving or of being loved, she became the one to whom I chose to confide my tragic fate. Chiefly my impending fate, of course. She was a well brought up girl of good family. She became both frightened and moved, and it was not long before she was prepared to comfort me in bed.

This was easier said than done, for we were both inexperienced.

However, we were absolutely determined to try. Armed with a bottle of cheap brandy we went by train in the middle of winter to the summer cottage that belonged to my girl-friend's parents. It was even colder inside than out.

We hunted out all the blankets and quilts in the house and piled them on to a bed. We then crept under this mountain of textiles without taking off any of our clothes except our trousers. We were wearing double woollen jumpers and thick stockings, but we still froze as the bed-clothes were icy. We lay pressed close together with a few dozen square centimetres of bare skin in direct contact.

There was nothing wrong with my erection.

In order to warm up inside we took a good pull at the brandy, and warmth radiated from our stomachs as from the sun.

In principle everything was in order.

I kissed her and embraced all her jumpers. She smelt of newly washed hair, naphthalene, and damp wool. I then moved my hand down to the bare spot and the contact with tufts of hair almost made me faint.

I took another good pull.

She said my hand was cold, she wondered if she would get inflammation of the bladder.

I gave her the bottle and told her that brandy was the right medicine for inflammation of the bladder. She took a pull, so did I to calm myself down a bit.

I stroked her hole with my finger, felt the moisture in it, and that was too much for me. I could not help myself but thoroughly soaked the two of us with sticky seminal fluid.

When she saw my dismay she asked what had happened. I told her and she said she wondered if we had come all this way for nothing.

I comforted her and said that all would be well in a moment. It was only excess pressure that had to be got rid of. All the same she was uneasy.

We took another pull while we waited for another erection with which to reach our goal.

It was not long before we could set to work again. I tried to steer it in, but then she pulled me up short, and said we mustn't make her pregnant.

Of course we'd thought of that and I had with me a dozen condoms, but first I wanted to try what it felt like without one. However, I realized that she was right. I could not guarantee that what had happened before would not happen again, so I dug out a rubber.

It took me some time to get the hang of how to unroll it. When at last I'd got the idea it proved impossible to get it on under all our coverings. I got quite sweaty with despair and exertion before I realized that it was no go. I should have to get out of bed.

The temperature in the room was minus thirty. I took a good pull at the brandy, and when it had pumped a bit of warmth into my veins, I leapt out of bed with the rubber at the ready, only to discover to my horror that my stand had withered and faded like yesterday's tulip. There was just enough left to make it possible to get the rubber on, but it was as wrinkled as Grandmother's silk stocking that I had worn at my nursery school.

I burst into tears of despair.

She pulled me back into bed and did all she could to comfort me. She said she was sure that now I would get inflammation of the bladder.

I thought up a new plan. As soon as my erection was what it should be, and it soon was, I would scramble out of bed and she should put on a new rubber. For one thing she would be handier at it, and for another my cock would certainly not go slack if she was doing it.

She said she did not think that a girl of good family ought to do things like that. I said she must if we were going to get anywhere. Think of the long way we'd come and the cold we'd endured. She took a pull at the brandy to get her courage up.

The plan succeeded and, with a sigh of relief and well enveloped, I was able to creep down to her again. The next difficulty was to get it in. I just could not. Our lengthy preparations and various mishaps had diverted her interest from the pleasurable aspect, and she had become quite dry. Lubricated rubbers did not exist at that time.

I pushed and shoved, groaned and sweated, and she laughed and cried, and in the end we had to give up. When we returned to town she was still inviolate though I'd carried on like a wrestler. Even violence had not enabled her to give herself. The thought that if we had been Adam and Eve we should still have been in Paradise did not comfort me one bit.

I realized that, like Napoleon, I had underestimated the cold of winter and the fact that it is an ally of the defender. My winter war was pretty unsuccessful too, though the person I attacked was as willing to surrender as Kuusinen's Terijoki government.* Nor was I going to say, as Mannerheim did when the next war began, that I would not sheathe my sword until Karelia was liberated. It was the one thing I wanted to do, whatever became of Karelia.

All these allusions to world politics in connection with an unsuccessful amorous episode might sound far-fetched were it not for the fact that the future course of our love affair was much affected by events in the World War. For me my love became a part of the war, it lived and died with the war. And so did my sweetheart whose name was Brita. Soon after peace was declared she died of cancer.

Her family had taken over where my father's grand-father had left off. He had helped to give the Finnish people its language and then he went mad. Her ancestors had used the opportunities that language offered to give the people an ideology, and as a result had grown wealthy. They also became aristocratic, and as hide-bound as the most expensive books published by their firm. They conducted themselves with great dignity and expressed themselves in empty phrases and quotations. This soon made them so unassailable and apart that ordinary people were seized by feelings of awe and deference.

They set the pattern for the educated Finnish upper-class style of life which is still warmly cherished by rectors of universities, directors of big banks, consultants and generals. In other words by those who have authority over the majority of the people, and therefore believe themselves to represent true democracy in the country.

* Kuusinen was a Finnish traitor who set up a government, which claimed to be the real government of Finland, on the Russian border at the start of the Winter War in 1938.

They had, of course, adopted the Finnish form of their name, and looked upon me with justifiable suspicion because I had a Finnish name from the start and could not use it as a means of manifesting my Finnishness. My girl friend, Brita, made great efforts to cultivate in me a proper national spirit by reading me poems by Koskenniemi and Hellaakoski while I cheerfully continued to paw her. She said that I was consumed by animal passions which were unworthy of a true patriot. Nevertheless, she agreed to another attempt and a successful defloration took place in my father's bed on Brändö.

I was very happy and promised to offer my life for my country. This thought also attracted me because it implied death and tragedy. It gave me an opportunity to exercise that bitter-sweet self-pity and sentimentality which I had learnt to confuse with strong feelings. The rapid advance of the Germans on all fronts also made it improbable that I should ever need to redeem my promise.

Everything looked fine until the Germans suddenly attacked the Russians, their only motive being the non-aggression pact. On that same day we too found ourselves at war.

How that happened I do not know. The Minister, who still came to visit my mother, always looked equally miserable, and never said now that he longed for Petroskoj* instead of for Monte Carlo. His love for Mother began to resemble his love for the Swedish Liberal Party. He knew that both had seen their best days, and that he would remain the last great lover of his kind, the chieftain who was a Swedish-Finnish giant.

It was clear that an epoch was over, and it is possible that the Minister would not have wanted to enter the war at all had it not been that Mannerheim, who led

* Petroskoj = Petrozavodsk on the west coast of Lake Onega, the capital of the Karelian Republic of the Soviet Union.

the enterprise, was Swedish. He never suggested, as did my eldest brother, that there was any question of imminent disaster any more than there was of future success. His characteristics were moderation, sense, and judgement, and if he contributed to the national catastrophe he certainly did so with the welfare of the Swedish settlements in view. Years of trial had not improved his digestion and his breath was not as irreproachable as his dark suit. But Mother's was not much better. After the armistice she had begun to drink beer laced with sleeping-pills. The Minister may have realized that peace did not suit Mother and made up his mind accordingly. It is certain that he acted for good reasons and after careful consideration.

The Prime Minister went still further and clearly thought that peace was not good for any patriot. This explains his enthusiasm when, on the outbreak of war, he went to ex-President Ståhlberg's home on Brändö and declared: 'Mr President, I have the honour to inform you that we, and the great German Republic are at war with the Soviet Union. And I give you my word that everything will be over in ten days.'

The Presidents and Prime Ministers of our Republic were in the habit of going to the old creator of our constitution to consult him and to ask his advice. President Paasikivi continued this practice until Ståhlberg had his first stroke after the war. But on this occasion it is obvious that the Prime Minister wanted congratulations not advice, and these the former President could not give.

When he told me of this episode long after the war his voice still shook with indignation. He had pointed to the door and said: 'Mr Prime Minister you have made a frightful mistake, I must ask you to leave my house.'

The Prime Minister had shuffled off, no doubt regretting that he had not said two weeks instead of **ten** days.

He was not the only person to be mistaken about the duration of the war. I was too. Our initial successes were so overwhelming that the assault had the same effect on youthful minds that gold has during a gold-rush. It was a question of getting there in time to help yourself to the glory.

The trouble was that I was too young. Classmates of mine reported for duty in the Waffen SS so that they would be able to help in taking Moscow. They wore a death's-head cockade in their caps and an eagle on their breasts. They were the commandos of the Second World War, and when they came back from Germany they would make Finland even freer than she had been before. The Germans were specialists at liberating people from democratic corruption.

During the summer vacation I managed to wheedle my way into an air-defence company which, led by its instructor Captain Guido Simberg, was going to hunt for paratroopers dropped behind our lines. We were sent to Sordavala and arrived immediately after it fell. I was able to see for myself what a mess the Russians left behind them. In the houses food was mouldering on the tables and the washing-up had not been done. It was obvious that the Slavs were a lower race than the Germanic peoples and the Finno-Ugrians, who at least wash themselves in their saunas every Saturday night.

We then marched through the autumn forest to the shores of Lake Ladoga and looking out over that great expanse of water that was fresh, not salt, seemed a fantastic experience to us. I bent down and touched the surface of the lake with my lips intending to drink the holy water that surrounded Valamo monastery. But it was also water that accepted atheists and gently rocked them on its waves, for when I raised my eyes a

93

fraction from the mirror of water I found myself staring straight into the eyeballs of a dead soldier who was floating about like a swollen French roll.

I spat out the water and went on spitting until I vomited. I was convinced that the dead man had polluted the whole lake. It struck me that the war also had its unaesthetic sides. If one dead body could drive the charm from one of the largest lakes in the world what would happen if we were obliged to kill two hundred million Russians?

Before I had time to stumble on any more dead bodies the vacation was over and I was sent back to school. I had nothing to embroider upon but the dead body in Lake Ladoga and I ended up by implying that we had fought a battle. In so far as his introverted gaze had nearly frightened the life out of me this was true. I comforted myself by thinking that if he had not been dead he would have come off worst anyhow, for I was not afraid of living people who were bathing.

At any rate I had almost been at the front and for the moment this was enough for Brita. She considered that she could still be accommodating on patriotic grounds.

I tried to get Father to prevail on General Kekoni, whom he met at the Stock Exchange Club, to arrange for me to go to the front, but Father was suddenly obstinate. He said he did not want to lose his only intelligent son. I was furious because he discredited the twins and because I thought I was more cunning than they were.

Nor did Mother succeed in interesting any of her old friends in the idea of taking me into their units. One said plainly that he wasn't going to be responsible for a late abortion. Mother was so annoyed that she kept away from all the officers she knew and struck up a friendship with a sergeant major. When he committed suicide after the great communal drinking-bout that followed the capture of Karhumäki she went the whole hog and married a private.

After that the Minister abandoned her. Is there anything more worthless than a private?

I had to stay on at school for a whole year before I finally succeeded in enlisting as a volunteer in Nyland's cavalry regiment, Mannerheim's own unit. I dreamed of riding into St. Petersburg and Moscow to the cheers of the liberated population.

But once again I was to be disappointed. The High Command of our defence forces had read in the papers of the great defeat the Polish cavalry had suffered against German tanks. Finland had neither enough horses nor men for such a splendid manifestation of courage, and so horses were exchanged for motor cycles which do not encourage exaggerated heroic deeds. Into the bargain I landed up in a machine-gun troop, which meant that I had to lug along a horribly heavy metal object which deprived a soldier's calling of its last vestige of romance.

I was wretchedly unhappy at Villmanstrand, and when I sat peeling potatoes or cleaning the lavatory with a tooth-brush I felt further from honour and heroism than ever before. One of the twins was at the Karelian isthmus and the other on the Murmansk railway, and what use was it to me that I was more intelligent than they were. If the war ended before I had time to take part everyone would look up to them, and no one would bother about me. Even my own children would sit on their uncles' knees and ask them to tell of their wartime exploits. I wrote one letter after another to the twins asking them to try to get me transferred to their units.

Finally my northern brother succeeded and glad at heart I travelled via Petroskoj to Karhumäki. From the station at Malus I walked the last kilometre to the battalion headquarters where I was to report. They sent me to the machine-gun company where I was greeted by my Company Commander with the following words: 'Devil take me, you look as if your mum had been fucked by a salt-herring through a keyhole.'

At last I stood face to face with the enemy I should hate for as long as the war lasted, indeed for the whole of my life.

I clicked my heels without answering and departed to my post in the front line. Though the Russians were hardly a hundred yards away I could not see them.

17

In trench warfare the private soldier sees about as much of the war as the crew of the atomic submarine, Nautilus, saw of the North Pole when they passed underneath it. If the engine had not throbbed they would never have known that the submarine was moving. Exploding shells and the coughing of machine-guns were the only indications we had that the dreariness of the wilderness was not buried for eternity in the holes where we sat scratching our lice bites. Death hung like an uncertain promise over our heads while at the same time it held us through fear, boredom, oppression, cold, filth, and bad food. Some might return from the war as heroes, none as victors.

War has only one end and that is death, and to describe war is to describe how soldiers die.

Well then. One of my friends got a bullet between his eyes just when he was telling me how he'd thought of a way to arrange for his transfer from the front line. There was a little hole at the base of his nose, but the whole of the back of his head had gone. One eye was turned inwards as if, in alarm, he was trying to see where his brains had got to.

My bunk-bedfellow had his stomach torn open by a long sliver of metal that looked like a Turkish sabre. In his surprise he tried to push back the bowels that were crawling out between his fingers. Before he had succeeded he was dead.

The corporal in my section died just as he was about to empty his fourth tankard of beer for the morning at the Picknick restaurant. That was twelve years and I can't say how many pints after the war. Two marriages had come to grief before his liver suddenly cancelled its contract.

A Knight of the Order of Mannerheim shot his wife and burnt her body in the yard outside his holiday cottage. He was just as cold-blooded in peace as in war. Death was his only argument.

The commander of the second battalion shot himself twenty-two years after the war because the women at the office of which he was boss, refused to stand to attention when he spoke to them.

The cavalry captain who took off his breeches and seduced my sister-in-law was found ten years later in a sand-pit in the harbour where he had frozen to death.

My brother, who was wounded four times and won four medals, had four thromboses and the fourth killed him soon after his fiftieth birthday.

The other brother, who could never understand the meaning of the war, never found any meaning in life after it either, and hanged himself from a water-pipe in his cellar before he was fifty.

Death never signed any peace treaty, it carried on its war to the last man. The real descriptions of war consist of death certificates and post-mortem reports. All other descriptions, despite their honest intentions, are false. Mailer, Linna, and Heller have all, against their will, created glorifying heroic epics, in which the survivors of war revel unsuspectingly.

War books deteriorate irretrievably into the pornography of violence. It is simply not possible to write a pure-hearted love-story the scene of which is a fifth class brothel. On the other hand it is perfectly possible to make sociological studies of war. War is like hard liquor, it does not reveal the truth, but it lets the friends of the devil loose.

I cannot remember getting a single letter from Father while I was at the front. He was too busy with his private war, the destruction of his own existence. His arguments were not unlike those of the politicians who had taken their country into the war. In his own eyes he was entitled to a gigantic realm of good fortune where there would be unlimited *lebensraum* for his strong, beautiful emotions. As he obstinately screened off the real reasons for his inability to create a life of harmony he saw his unimaginative, bourgeois wife as the dragon at the gates of paradise. Consequently he attacked her in the most demoniacal way his self-absorption could devise, that is by forcing her to look on helplessly at his ac-celerating decline. No rational arguments could persuade him to give up, he was possessed by the same unreason-able egoism as the people who, during the war, saw total extinction as the only alternative to victory. National leaders who enter a war for the sake of the nation end up sacrificing the nation for their own sake. I can see that my father did not want to upset me by telling me what a bad time he was having.

He did not write to the twins either. But they probably did not think this remarkable. The only things he ever felt obliged to communicate to them were his reproaches and his contempt, and when they did not receive these my brothers must obviously have thought that he was pleased with their efforts.

Indeed, he might very well have been. His sons con-ducted themselves admirably, all but the youngest who was his pride.

The upbringing the twins had had was geared to military life. From the time they were little they had been hounded, insulted, and treated unjustly, and they had been forced to put up with it. Their new circum-stances were familiar, indeed, paradoxically enough, secure. No demands were made here for individual contributions or the ability to criticize independently. No one here put them under pressure by expecting too much of them. And they had been nurtured on fear.

At home they were afraid of Father, but were forbidden to oppose him.

In war you were afraid of the enemy, but the whole idea was that you should oppose him. The war presented them with their first opportunity to let off steam, to develop and mature. The one who had never got through secondary school became a lieutenant, and the other, who from his primary schooldays had spent two years in every class, became a sergeant.

Everyone admired them. They were praised by their comrades and their superiors. The warmth that had been cooped up in them was released by comradeship and a feeling of being accepted. The tragedy for them, as for so many other people in our society, was that the war offered them the only human contacts and the only memorable experiences they ever had in their lives. When the war proved to be a fiasco they had nothing to turn to.

But the youngest son was a disappointment. Father's own little genius, the artful dodger whom Mother had hoped would be a cavalry captain or a gynaecologist never became more than a private, and hardly that. At the non-commissioned officers' school he was almost bottom because he could not drill closed ranks without roaring with laughter. When drilling a smile is an offence and a laugh unforgivable. Deadly seriousness is a prerequisite for the proper functioning of an authoritarian system. And that is not all. In spite of the fact that he had belonged to the defence corps and had volunteered for the front he was critical and demanded explanations for orders whose only explanation was that they were orders. He had no future in the war.

That was why his Company Commander decided to

make an end of him. Not to believe in victory is treason, but mocking the military system is worse than being a deserter. And the Captain of the machine-gun company, who was also the second in command of the battalion, had been lifted as high by the system as it was possible for a man to get. He had unlimited power over two hundred souls. He might be given a dressing-down if they showed a lack of enthusiasm for killing, but never if they willingly went to their death. If he wanted to kill someone he could. This could be achieved by so many means that the act was almost uninteresting. He therefore chose the most complicated procedure, which was also the one that gave him the most amusement. He sought by mental torture to break down the young volunteer's self-esteem, to force him to choose between murder and suicide.

It was not long before I found out his intentions, though fortunately I, like my brothers, had learnt something from Father. I was able to divine the motive behind his merciless persecution. He was hunted by the demons of fear, and his awareness of the approaching catastrophe made him challenge fate by offering her two alternatives, both equally bad. He wanted to force me to take over his fear and free him from it by committing suicide in his place. The alternative was that in sheer desperation, I should shoot him and save him from having to do it himself.

He often begged and prayed me to do it. He put the pistol in my hand and told me to pull the trigger. But I never did, for that would have been like playing Russian roulette. If I had pulled the trigger and there had been no bullet in the chamber he would have been able to accuse me of attempted murder, and I should have been entirely at his mercy.

As if that mattered anyway. When he forced me to sit in his bunker all night long to keep him company while he drank, he could have accused me of anything. There were no witnesses, and my word against his was valueless. He could have shot me like a rat, and no one would have made him answer for it.

But he was afraid and when he was drunk his fear assumed enormous proportions. The hounds of madness grabbed at the nerve-ends trailing behind him, and he confused his own terror with the terror of war. He never dared go near the front when he was sober. It was only when he was alone with me and could torment me without hindrance that he became calm, sometimes almost happy. Then a wave of warmth would break over him and with tears in his eyes he would tell me that I was like his little brother who had fallen. And because I was like him I too must die, to right a wrong.

I have been accused of individualism, and of an inability to fit into a collective. This is true. But individualists have characteristics that make them suitable for crucifixion. I believe my comrades had reason to thank me for diverting from them a good part of the madness which would otherwise have been vented upon the whole company. I began to understand the purpose of adjutants. They are the fragile lightning-conductors for those outbreaks of total insanity bound to occur among commanding officers left alone to bear such inhuman responsibility.

I fought for my life and I was neither optimistic nor brave. I did all I could to save myself, and at the same time I mobilized all my strength to ward off his attacks. I was fighting against an enemy I was forbidden to oppose. I was being forced to carry my brothers' struggle against their unreasonable father a step further.

But I received no help from my brother who was in command of the platoon and of the machine-gun post where I was stationed. He told me to take things easy. I asked him if I was to take things easy when the

Captain tried to kill me? He said I ought to be happy. While I was with the Captain the Russians couldn't kill me. He also said that he was sure the Captain liked me, if not why did he ask me to sit with him? I said that he didn't ask he commanded, and that he didn't like me he hated me. My brother said I was making it up. I admitted that perhaps he did not hate me, he hated himself through me. Then my brother said that he could see that I didn't know what I meant myself. In a word, I had the wind up and wanted to get away from the front. Why had I come here as a volunteer? It was too late now.

I asked him if he wasn't worried by the injustices of our Company Commander? Every man returning from leave was obliged to bring him a bottle of *brännvin*,* otherwise he would have to wait in vain for his next leave. And every time the army ration of *brännvin* was issued a wooden screwcapful from every bottle went to the Captain. He was never without *brännvin*.

I asked if the Captain had the right to open his men's letters and censor them? Two of his soldiers had complained to their member of parliament, Demari's *causerie* writer Jahvetti, and as punishment he had forced them to ride backwards in front of the company, while he announced that he was their God and Jahvetti. All complaints should be addressed to him.

I asked if it was right that the Captain should appear dead drunk in the lines after a battle and try to slit open the stomach of a wounded prisoner with a knife? He would have done it too if a sergeant from my brother's platoon had not threatened to shoot him if he touched the prisoner.

* *Brännvin* A mixture of ethyl alcohol ($35-55\%$), water and flavouring. Often called *sprit* = spirits. Once the cheapest and still the most common form of spirits drunk in Scandinavia.

My brother looked startled and said that he hoped the Captain was so drunk that he did not remember what had happened, otherwise the sergeant might find himself court-martialled.

I asked him if he had no thought for the prisoner and he asked what had happened to him. I told him that he had fainted from fear and everyone thought he was dead. So they had thrown him out into the cold, and the following morning he was really dead. The rats had eaten his nose, his eyes, and his cheeks, but there were tracks in the snow which indicated that he had crawled a few metres. My brother said that wasn't the Captain's fault, it was his nerves, he drank too much, just like Father. And anyhow, not all Company Commanders were the same, he was an exception.

I said that this might be so, but the system was such that it didn't stop these exceptions from getting to the top. The whole damned army was bloody rotten.

My brother's face was sad. He had looked forward to having me in his unit so that I could see from all his medals how well he was doing. Now I was indirectly accusing him of being 'bloody rotten'. His brotherly love was hard pressed, and I have no doubt he lost confidence in me. He gave up cheating at poker when I was looking on. He was afraid that with my inexplicable passions for right, I might no longer respect his rank as an officer, but might oblige him to show his hand, which would have meant a sudden end to an easy way of getting money for his leave.

To punish me he climbed up on to the parapet of the trench. A Russian sentry aimed a shot at him. He indicated with a twig that it had passed him on the left. The second shot went past him on the right, and this too he indicated with a twig. Then he jumped down to shelter. He had shown his contempt for death and given me a demonstration of courage which he doubtless thought compensated for minor abuses of power, and ought to make me ashamed that I had ever dared to criticize those in command.

Besides, if I had been up to much I should have been selected for an officers' training course. Perhaps after all I wasn't really worth having, lucky that I was only his half-brother. This is what I imagined he was thinking, and I searched my soul to discover whether he mightn't be right.

It was perfectly plain that I did not dare to climb on to the parapet and play at being a target. Nor was I as trusting as the country lads in my company. They were all at least two years older than I was, but they thought that war was like frost, it came when it came. Nor did they ever doubt the necessity of fighting. It was a case of defending your fatherland, that is, your father's fields. They would never have believed what an agricultural expert told them, they were far too conservative for that, but they trusted military experts implicitly, and went into an attack without a murmur, however meaningless their orders might be. If the operation failed and half of them were killed, it was the frost taking its toll again. God and their commanders were not to blame for what had happened, since both were on our side. In the words of the Field Marshal, they were incomparable soldiers.

My Company Commander said I was the worst soldier in the Finnish army.

A General I know, who is an expert on military politics, says that he has come to the conclusion that pacifists and others who slander war have, without exception, proved to be cowards and failures as soldiers.

This fits me exactly.

What surprises me is that this General, along with all the other soldiers who took part in the war, didn't become a pacifist too. People who have lost a war could reasonably regard themselves as failures. But the General doesn't agree. It is even impossible to convince him that we lost. He says that the army was undefeated when the armistice was signed. He is like a dazed boxer who protests that his second has thrown in the sponge at the very moment he was about to land a knock-out punch.

I was such a bad soldier that after the battle of Stalingrad I said that we should lose the war.

My brother said that we most certainly should not. He had been to a staff briefing the day before and the Colonel had said that we should win. Who would be likely to know better, the Colonel, who was in contact with Headquarters, or I, an ordinary private?

I said that of course the Colonel knew better. He knew what the General had said, and the General knew what the Field Marshal had said, and the Field Marshal knew what the Führer had said. And he had said that victory was ours.

'But if Hitler asks me what I think I shall tell him that we shall get it in the neck,' I said.

It was an impious thing to say and very rightly I was called before the Company Commander to answer for it. For once in the middle of the day. He looked at me with a furrowed brow and asked if I admitted I was a communist? I answered honestly that I knew that our enemies in the trenches opposite ours were communists, though admittedly against their will, but for the rest I had no idea what a communist was. In my family we had even avoided the word socialist.

My Company Commander asked if I had said we should lose the war.

I agreed that I had and asked whether I could possibly be wrong?

He filled a tumbler with *brännvin* and pushed it over to me. 'Drink,' he said.

I took the glass and drank. The stuff was warm and made me feel sick. Tears came into my eyes, but I got it all down, and instantly a hot wave broke over my stomach.

My Company Commander gave me an odd look, took the glass and filled it again to the brim. 'Take a pull on the other leg too,' he said.

I knocked back the second glass in one. It was easier this time. The hot wave swept up to my head and broke over my eyes, so that the Captain became fuzzily soft and harmless.

My Company Commander told me to go back to my post. I was undernourished and in such poor shape that two full glasses had made me very drunk. I heard the birds singing and I heard the bullets from a machine-gun salvo sing as they flew past, and the bullets were like the birds, they avoided me and I did not need to duck. I heard the bullets change into a woodpecker tapping a tree-trunk and I tried to catch a glimpse of him, but then the tree slowly divided as if the bullets had split it in two. In surprise I looked at another tree which also split in two. All the trees became two trees.

A dizzy feeling of power came over me when I realized that I could split a tree in two just by looking at it, and that the bullets could not touch me. I was clearly in a unique position to make a decisive contribution to the war. I hugged my rifle tightly as I ran the last bit to the communication trench and on to my position in the forward trench. Once there I scrambled out and initiated a single-handed attack upon the enemy. Shouting and cheering I stormed forward towards the barbed-wire fence and the minefield behind it. But I can't have been as nimble on my feet as I thought, for I hadn't taken many steps before the sentry caught hold of me and flung me back into the trench. A couple of sharp bursts from an anti-tank gun were the last things I heard before I fell asleep with my cheek pressed against the sand in the bottom of the trench.

After this episode our Company Commander left me in peace. I was no longer ordered to his bunker to be tormented throughout the night. And I got my leave when it was due.

When I returned to the front I had with me a bottle of good cognac for my Captain, my Company Commander. He accepted it and thanked me without moving a muscle.

I have tried to puzzle out for more than thirty years what that bottle of cognac represented.

Kindly feelings towards the torturer because he had ceased to torment me?

An elegant thank you for attempted murder?

An awareness deep down of a shameful understanding?

Triumph over a victory?

But in that case what victory? Violence and oppression breed feelings reminiscent of rats, and rats want to leave a sinking ship. We knew that the hour of reckoning was near, and if he helped me to survive until then it was up to me to forget what had gone before.

Shortly afterwards I was temporarily appointed map-maker at Brigade Headquarters.

18

Volunteering for the front might easily be interpreted as an act of bravery on my part. It wasn't at all. Primarily it was a display of childishness and secondly it needs very little courage to do as others do.

On the other hand to take your fate into your own hands and to be false to the collective ideal is a real test. The courage needed to desert, after careful deliberation, is so great that it should make the medals on any hero's breast tremble like the leaves of a lakeside elder.

It is setting yourself up against the very standards by which courage is judged. Courage that complies with the rules only occurs in the service of those in authority, and the quality of this courage depends on the degree of self-sacrifice which loyalty demands. The most brilliant examples of courage are those shown when you rescue your leader from mortal danger. As when my friend's ancestor gave the king his horse on the battle-field and had to lose his own life. Or to rush, with the national revenue in a suitcase, through a hail of bullets to a helicopter standing ready to take off with the Prime Minister and the Government on board. Such courage borders on madness as there will be no one left in the country to distribute medals.

By the same token cowardice is lack of loyalty. It is cowardly not to believe in Government propaganda. It is cowardly not to fight to the last man. It is cowardly to give up. It is cowardly to run away. It is cowardly to interpret a retreat as a retreat. It is cowardly to assess a hopeless situation correctly. If courage has nothing to do with common sense, common sense has altogether too much to do with cowardice.

In every intellectual lurks a deserter. That is why no responsible government is willing to spend too much money on education and culture.

I thought that because I had gone into the war as a volunteer I had the right to decide when to get out of it. Especially as the President was said to be running to a wise woman to learn how the miserable war would end.

My maternal grandmother told me that her cousin, Professor Yrjö Hirn, had sat in his rocking chair tugging his beard and said: 'Things are bound to go wrong when the President is a spiritualist and the Prime Minister a sportsman.'

I had no horse to give either to the President or to the Prime Minister, but they would have been welcome to an old Maxim machine-gun if they had cared to show themselves on the Karelian isthmus during the great offensive of that last summer. But they never showed up.

On the other hand I saw Regimental Commanders rushing about recklessly on the roads calling to their two thousand boys who had left them in the lurch. And I saw the boys whole, in halves, in bits, strewn all over the place, and I saw the wave of panic that no military police could stem by shooting down fleeing soldiers. Panic is the fear that disregards death. It is essential to keep a cool head and not let yourself panic.

It was somewhere near Summa, the honourable battle-field of the Winter War that I settled my account with the war. At first it had seemed to be an exciting adventure, but it had turned out to be a miserable mistake, both for me and for President Risto Ryti, who really ought to have known better.

I had certainly tried everything that seemed feasible. I had applied time after time to become a front-line draughtsman, but I had been turned down, ironically enough, because I could not draw in the manner of Soviet socialist realism which Finland's High Command regarded as the only correct style.

I had asked both Father and Mother to get me moved, but in vain. The Ministers and Generals whom Father met at the Stock Exchange Club had already come to the conclusion that every man was needed at his post if they were to have any chance of playing billiards at the Club in future. And Mother had married a private so no commissioned officer now listened to her. Her marriage had also released the Minister who had loved her so much from his obligations. His love, which had brought her misfortune, had now been transferred to the nation and the story looked like being repeated. The fate of individuals no longer concerned him.

In fact there was surprisingly little interest in what was likely to happen to me. The discovery upset me. I had been under the impression that the world revolved round me. One discovery led to another. Not only did the world revolve round me it only existed through me. If I got a bullet in my head the world would be annihilated. I was responsible for this world which was kept in being by my consciousness. The war was a nightmare that I was having in my sleep. Instead of dying I must wake up.

At that time the answer to every problem lay in weapons: gun-powder embodied wisdom. But it also presented the greatest technical problem.

A Soviet ground support plane flying at a low altitude had hunted me several times round a large stone in a field by shooting at me with a machine-gun both from the front and the rear. This personal interest in my farewell to life struck me as almost flattering in that roaring inferno where no one seemed to care about his fellows.

I thought of Mother. She wrote a letter every day.

She cared about me. As always difficulties had made her grow. The woman who had abandoned me when she could reach me was always with me now that she could no longer take me in her arms.

I wondered what she would say if I fell in battle.

As the situation was then it seemed sheer madness to sacrifice one's life for a cause that was already lost. The battalion was smashed to splinters, I had no idea where my company might be if indeed it still existed. I had not slept for seven days. I was tired.

Seven cows were grazing in the field. The plane that hunted me brought them down one by one. When one was killed the others went on grazing calmly, they munched up the juicy green grass until the moment they died. No fear, no panic. They were brave. Nothing in the world was as brave as our Finnish cattle.

If one shot oneself in the arm at close range there would be a black smudge round the wound that a doctor might misinterpret, and doctors had as little sympathy with deserters as parsons. A nervous breakdown was an acceptable reason for removing a man to the home front only if he was in the High Command. If an ordinary soldier went mad through fear it did not matter, for fear was a normal reaction in war and the lunatic was only normal to an unusually high degree. Everyone except homosexuals and sodomites was free to offer their lives on the field of glory.

I placed my arm behind the trunk of a young birch, took careful aim, and executed the tree.

I was so numbed by weariness that I did not feel any pain when the bullet went through my arm. The black smudge was on the white skin of the birch and my wound was clean and tidy. The bullet that went through my flesh deflowered me. A shameful deed had made a man of me.

I had taken my fate into my own hands.

19

One day during the war one of our two magnificent
warships had to pass through the Straits of Pargas.
Suddenly the officer on the bridge felt an irresistible
desire to see what would happen if he charged through
the narrow channel at full speed.

What happened was that the water surged high up
the banks and the ship touched bottom, but managed to
plough through from sheer impetus.

The war had been like that, splendid and daring. All
hell might have been let loose. That it was not shows
that those who embarked on the war had not been
entirely wrong. It might have gone well.

The ground swell that had washed the shore was
annoying. It had smashed a number of things to bits and
carried off quite a lot of goods and chattels. In return it
had left behind sludge and piles of rubbish that no one
wanted to see on their shores.

Consequently a number of people said it was damned
silly to run a man-of-war through the Straits of Pargas
at top speed. Others said that it was still more foolish
to take a man-of-war out into the open sea. There, never
having caught a glimpse of the enemy, she ran onto a
mine off Utö and capsized and sank with the loss of
everyone and everything on board.

People still argue about which manœuvre was the
more insane instead of discussing Finland's total insanity
in ever equipping herself with immensely expensive
men-of-war that served no useful purpose. But apparently

when insanity reaches senseless proportions it becomes patriotism which may not be criticized, except by revolutionary elements, among whom you could not count Father.

Father did not criticize the war when it began nor when it ended. It was characteristic of him that he never complained. He accepted the blows of fate as personal trials. War, crises, and prohibition were all directed against him to prevent him living as a gentleman. He saw the patterns of his life ruffled as Archimedes did his circles, and he too was prepared to die for them rather than attempt to find new meaning in a world of ruins. He ordered his ex-libris from the artist Björn Landström, and for its motif he chose two broken pillars from the Acropolis. But his wife found it difficult to accept him as a ruin. Bacchus can be as ruthless as Mars. Both tempt people with majestic visions which later change to misery and suffering. And in times of crisis the cost of going under in as grand a manner as possible was not small. As the price of *brännvin* constantly rose and there was no work for an architect, money became the all-pervading problem in my home on Brändö.

Consequently, when my brothers returned from the front they found themselves the owners of a quite fantastic wardrobe. Their mother had left a little money which they were to inherit when they came of age. But Father rightly considered that their chances of returning alive from the war were not very great, and he therefore succeeded in persuading his friend the district judge, who was trustee for the money, to agree to a transaction that would be beneficial to all parties. Father took the money plus the risk of inflation, and in exchange the boys got the whole of Father's valuable wardrobe consisting of innumerable suits in the best English tweed and innumerable shoes made by Bally of Switzerland.

A wardrobe like this at a time when shoes and clothes were made of paper was certainly priceless. The only trouble was that the twins were a head taller than Father and that the shoes were two sizes too small. Moreover, Father continued to use them.

To remedy this miscalculation my parents hit on the splendid idea that Father's wife should adopt the twins. By this means they would, in course of time, inherit her money at least. The boys gratefully accepted the arrangement and thought that their stepmother was treating them jolly well, just like an elder sister.

She was indeed not many years older than they were, but she lived many years longer, as good, considerate people usually do in a wicked world.

Her life with Father had not been a bed of roses. He had taken her youth as he took his brim-full drinks, now the time had come for her to present her bill. She was therefore as interested as he was in getting hold of what money there was left. And that belonged to Father's mother.

My grandmother shuffled slowly about in thick socks through her rooms in the flat under Father's, watering her flowers and wiping the dust from her dear old odds and ends, among which was a marble bust of herself. It had been made by her friend Valter Runeberg, and represented a very beautiful young woman with a classical profile. If Mother was designed for the twentieth century, Grandmother was created for the romantic classicism of the nineteenth. She was even more beautiful in her old age. The years had chiselled her features with a hand as sensitive as Runeberg's, and her dignified Red Indian face was framed by a snow-white mass of shining hair that looked like a bridal veil. She still lived proudly in the last century, which she preserved in her flat. She never troubled herself about the world outside, her pictures and her memories kept her alive.

No one can say for certain whether she was quite happy or had everything she wanted.

Fearing fire when the city was bombed she climbed into the bath. And there she sat until the alert was over. She would not go into the air-raid shelter for fear of being buried under the building along with Tom, Dick, and Harry. She had hidden her silver in the wood stack in the courtyard. Her legs had grown worse from sitting in cold water.

As a result of this hardship she had great open sores on her legs which served well enough as a reason for Father and his wife to get her into hospital for proper care. Nobody felt it necessary to worry about the fact that she did not want to go into hospital, for it was obvious that a person who hid her silver in the wood stack did not know what was best for her. So she was taken to Stengård and put into a ward for chronic invalids.

Her son had done his duty. Alcohol does not only demoralize those who drink, but also those who are obliged to look on. No one protested about this swift and gentle manner of putting Grandmother to death.

She lay in a bed with white sheets, and she begged us with tears in her eyes to water her plants. She then withered as fast as a flower that has not been watered. Within a week she was dead.

Grandmother died at a most convenient moment. The chapel at the cemetery on Brändö had just got a new crucifix and the parson, the Rev. Werner Wirén, who conducted the burial service, spoke so long and so warmly of the new crucifix, that the members of the general public who were present returned to their homes convinced that Grandmother had donated it to the parish.

Father was also in such a radiant good temper at the funeral coffee party that everyone could see how hard Grandmother's long illness had been for him, and how relieved he was that her suffering was now at an end.

He was at last able to re-establish his position. As a first step he sent Grandmother's portrait-bust as a gift to Prince Eugen, to be incorporated in his royal art Collection at Waldemarsudde outside Stockholm.

Though the Prince had been a good friend of Grandfather's his letter of thanks, to Father's great disappointment, was signed by his private secretary. That was not a thing you could show to people at the Stock Exchange Club, and there was no hope of getting Grandmother back, either in the flesh or in marble.

He decided to be wiser about her money. He had seen three wars, one depression, and one Prohibition Act. He had seen most of the things that were expensive and holy shattered to fragments, and he had learnt that whatever course the world takes the price of spirits is bound to go up. He therefore invested all his available ready money in alcohol, and laid down a large stock in his capacious larder. There was plenty of room there due to the crying lack of provisions. The only things already on the shelves were a few tins of pickled pike.

By dint of complicated calculations, which extended both backwards and forwards in time, he came to the conclusion that in ten years he would be a rich man. When his wife asked him to go to the dairy he refused, saying that the milk would be too expensive if the value of his time was taken into account. His wife then went to the dairy herself, but she never came back with the milk.

Father was obliged to begin to drink what he had in store in the larder, and his calculations proved to have been so far out that he had to buy the last bottle he drank before he died. He bought it at Svalbogatan in Sörnäs at an exorbitant price.

20

War is the death-throe of an epoch and peace is its
burial. It is a sin to sacrifice young men to old men
weary of life. For the old there is no victory and no
defeat, for both victory and defeat are the beginning of
something new. And they fought to prevent change,
they wanted to preserve the world as they knew it,
though the world had changed. When Father looked out
of his window he could see Kronberg fjord and Sveaborg.
Nothing had changed. He could see the street and its
tram-lines and the little park on the other side of the
street. Nothing had changed. He could see the forest
through the other window. Everything was the same.

And yet his friend, Jarl Hemmer, had put a bullet
through his own heart, sitting in a chair in the Poet's
Home at Borgå.* The sufferings and misfortunes of man-
kind had affected him deeply, and he had realized his
own impotence. Then, through the Oxford Movement,
he had turned to God who is all-powerful. But God is
also liberal-minded and permits much evil. Hemmer
could not understand that and his death was a protest
against both God and man.

When the news of Hemmer's death reached him Father
took out the poem his friend had written for his fiftieth
birthday, and weeping, read it aloud. He had not met

* The Poet's Home at Borgå is a house belonging to the
Swedish Literary Society which uses it as a grace and favour
home for distinguished authors.

Hemmer for many years, but he saw a black hole in the place where Hemmer should have been, and it frightened him.

And the bed where his wife should have lain was empty. Here too was a great black hole which he could no longer fill. He lay helplessly on his back and drank *brännvin* and masturbated like a little boy to drive away the solitude. He was the devil's friend, but that did not prevent the devil from making trouble.

The hardest blow was when he was politely but firmly informed that his presence was no longer desired at the Stock Exchange Club, which he had helped to found himself. It was as if the earth had split open and he stood staring down into a great black hole. The 'lost generation' of the First World War had become the sottish generation of the Second.

Nothing was as it had been.

The twins, who lived in the room next to his, told him, when they collided at the bathroom door, that he would drink himself to death if he did not stop soon. 'That's the idea,' he told them, and locked himself in his room.

I could see his feet and half his body through the glass door. I could see his hands fumbling between his legs, and I was almost sick with disgust when I discovered that my father hungered for sex. It was indecent at his age. The intolerance that had surrounded me, and which I had fought tooth and nail, had made me intolerant. The glass door was transformed into a mirror which scornfully showed me my future . . . for indeed we had much in common. I always felt that strongly when I visited him at Kammio,* where he went to recover between the bouts of heavy drinking that occurred with increasing frequency. We could sit holding hands for a

* A mental hospital.

long time in silence. When only we two were together in a room there was no friction between us. It was in relation to other people that we fought on opposite sides. And his side no longer existed. He was alone, dying, fearing death, yet still trying time after time to approach it with the help of spirits. But he folded up before he reached the goal and then one of his sons transported him to hospital. When he knew which day he would be able to leave he rang up Brändö Casino and ordered a window table for that evening.

There were summer days too, sea and sailing-boats. But there were no intimate conversations, only intimate silences. This brilliant drawing-room lion of the Twenties lay in his bed and did not know what to say to his son. His anguish, the weight of his accumulated experiences, he could not ease by confiding in me, or even by complaining of his misery.

'My hat has three corners. If it has not three corners it is not my hat.'

I hated his weakness and I hated his courage, and I loved his weakness and I loved his courage, and his loneliness filled me with terror.

I wished he would die.

The women who had left him must have sensed that he was dying, for both of them turned up with their demands and their wishes. My mother came to make things up, to assure herself that all was forgotten and forgiven. For the sake of the son they had in common. She herself had forgotten all her wrongs. But when they had sat for an hour drinking *brännvin* in the bedroom they had once shared she began to remember them again. Nor was it long before they parted, drunk and in anger, never to meet again.

When the next wife arrived Father was already drunk. She said she wanted some pictures, and he said take what you want. She told him she needed furniture for the flat she had rented, and he said take all you need. She had a van waiting outside, which showed that she had never doubted his generosity, and she took all she needed. Among other things she took the sofa on which my brother was lying reading in his room. But he did not complain, for he thought she was splendid. She had always been just and defended the twins against Father.

Against their father.

One day when Father was in hospital I went to Brändö with a frightful hangover and looked into the pantry to see if I could find anything to drink. I saw two eggs, and I took them instead of spirits. I ate them raw and soon felt very much better. I was glad that I had not gone on drinking. Then I forgot the eggs.

But Father did not. He rang me up as soon as he got home and accused me of stealing. I was furious with him for having the face to bring up such a petty matter, even if it wasn't easy to get hold of eggs at that time. I banged down the receiver before he had finished. A moment later he rang again. I asked my maternal grandmother to answer and, if it was him, to say that I was not at home. After that I never spoke to him again, and I am forever plagued by the thought that I don't know what he wanted to say. Perhaps there was something else he wanted to mention besides those two damned eggs. Perhaps he wanted to say that he loved me, that he needed me. How do I know?

He was entirely alone when he died. Looking in at the glass door you could see his feet as usual. If you could have woken him up you'd have thought he had been asleep. But he did not wake when my brother banged on the door. So my brother broke open the door and found him lying with his mouth open like a crater from which the blood had gushed out and congealed, like brown lava, over the slopes of his body and his bed. Down in the valley, on the floor, lay an empty bottle of *brännvin*, and his rigid hand was holding another bottle of which he had drunk half.

My brother telephoned me and his twin brother and told us not to come. He did not want us to see what he had seen. It was as if he guessed that a dreadful death is even more tempting than frightening. You can never free yourself from it.

There is not much more to tell.

According to the doctor he had been dead for thirty-six hours. But the proprietor at Brändö Casino swore that it was hardly twenty-four since he had been there trying to buy a bottle. As he was clearly in need of it the proprietor had not sold him one. He had then taken a taxi to the black market in Svalbogatan, where he bought his last bottle from a charitable pedlar of illicit liquor who sold to anyone who had money.

Only we three brothers took his urn to the grave. We had a taxi from the crematorium to Brändö cemetery. I sat in the middle with the urn and the twins sat one on either side. I was smoking a cigarette. The column of ash on the cigarette grew longer. I lifted the lid of the urn and knocked the ash into it.

My brothers saw what I did but said nothing.

I did not know why I did it.

Afterword

The setting of this book is Finland in the 1920s and '30s, a time when the country was torn by feuds of language and class, which can best be understood against a background of Finnish history.

Linguistically Finland is quite distinct in Scandinavia. The Finnish language, spoken by all but a tiny minority of her people, belongs to the Finno-Ugrian family, comprising Finnish, Hungarian, Estonian and Lappish, and bears no relation whatever to the languages of the other Scandinavian countries. Swedish is spoken by about 6% of Finns, and the people who speak it are known as Finno-Swedes, or Swedish-speaking Finns. These are the people who are the butt for Tikkanen's scorn.

The Swedes first came to Finland in numbers in the twelfth century and settled in the western and southern parts of the country, where they are still most numerous today. They found there a political vacuum: a people organized in small communities, without centralized government or monarchy, in need of allies to help defend them against marauders from East and West.

Until the seventeenth century Finland was a province of Sweden with considerable independence. Internal affairs were largely decided in Finland and in Finnish, but as the country developed, increasing numbers of administrators, army officers, and merchants were recruited from Sweden, and Swedish became the dominant language among the upper class. Under Gustav 11 (1611–32) greater efforts were made to impose conformity with Sweden, and the Finnish language declined still further.

After the Russian invasion of Finland in the nineteenth century, Alexander I declared the country to be an autonomous Grand Duchy, and the constitution and legal system remained as they had been under the Swedes. For the first few decades of Russian rule Swedish also remained the dominant language of governmental, legal and cultural affairs. With the spread of literacy in the 1840s, however, came the demand that Finnish should be given equal status with Swedish. The publication in 1835 of the *Kalevala* – the so-called 'Finnish epic', best known to us through the music of Sibelius – had made the Finns aware that they had a literary heritage of their own, and a language of which they could be proud. Finnish was not given equal status until 1863, and although twenty years were allowed for the change neither language was specified for use in the higher offices of government.

This reform was most seriously threatened by some Swedish-speaking Finns, but by 1905, when Finnish autonomy had ceased to exist, Swedish-Finns and Finnish-Finns were welded together by bitter hatred of Russia, and their language feud was forgotten.

Immediately after the outbreak of the 1914 War Finnish activists made plans to liberate Finland from Russia, though not all their countrymen supported a military solution. In some quarters it was hoped that the Western Powers would prevail on Russia to restore Finnish autonomy peacefully, for the link between the two countries had certain advantages; a number of Finns were employed on defence work, and Russian orders kept Finnish industry busy.

After the Russian revolution internal dissension in Finland escalated. All factions in Finnish politics wanted independence, but whereas the bourgeois parties wished to preserve the Swedish form of government still in force, the left-wing socialists wanted a new form on the Russian model.

In the autumn elections of 1917 the socialists lost their majority and revolutionary activity increased. The activists' reply was the formation of a corps of National Guards, with which they intended to drive the Russians out of Finland. The revolutionary socialists promptly formed their own corps of Red Guards, armed with weapons obtained from the Russian troops. A general strike was called and there were clashes between the two corps.

This was the position on 4 January, 1918 when Finland's independence was recognized by Russia, Germany, France and Sweden. The bourgeois government in Helsinki under the leadership of General Mannerheim was planning to expel the Russian troops, still not withdrawn by Lenin, without German help. But, on the night of 18 January, just as he was disarming the Russian garrisons in the north, the Red signal of revolt flared from the Workers' Headquarters in Helsinki. Some members of the legal government fled to Vasa, which became the centre of White Finland. The Socialist People's Commission took command of Helsinki. After their defeat in April 1918, the Red leaders fled to Russia and set up the Finnish Communist Party, which was later to play such an ignominious role in the Winter War.

The civil war did not last long, but it was fought with great ferocity and left deep scars. It was largely a class war with linguistic overtones. There were representatives of both language groups on each side, but mostly the leaders of the Whites were Swedish-speaking Finns. The Twenties and Thirties were periods of considerable antagonism between the two groups.

In the 1919 elections the Social Democrats, who had stood aside in the civil war, won 40% of the seats. The liberal politician, Ståhlberg, was elected President of the new republic, and did what he could to reconcile both sides. In 1920 communist expression was permitted in the press, and a party calling itself 'The Socialist Working People's Party' made its appearance. It won 14% of the votes in the 1922 elections, but was banned from parliamentary activity in 1923. It did not finally go underground until the beginning of the Thirties when it was made illegal under the Communist Laws. This proscription was no doubt in part a result of the extreme right-wing Lapua movement to which Tikkanen refers on p. 47, when he says that President Ståhlberg was kidnapped by an 'element in the population guaranteed to be patriotic'. Ståhlberg was suspected by the Lapua movement of being too liberal.

After being driven underground, and until the outbreak of the Second World War, the communists in Finland transferred their electoral support to the Social Democrats, now the party of the opposition.

In the Twenties Swedish speakers held a disproportionate number of important positions in governmental, cultural and economic life, but the Finnish speakers fought vigorously for their rights and by the mid-Thirties they had gained positions of importance proportionate to their numbers. At that time Swedish speakers numbered about 10% of the population, and Swedish in practice became the *second* language.

After 1935 Finland's economic recovery was rapid, but her attempts to assert her neutrality failed. The Russians feared her military weakness and warned her in 1935 that, if war broke out between Russia and other great powers, the Red Army would occupy Finland – and that this would take six days.

In 1939, after the Russo–German non-aggression pact, Russia demanded territorial concessions in the Karelian isthmus, and a naval base at Hankö at the entrance to the Gulf of Finland. Against the advice of Mannerheim these demands were refused. In October mobilization was ordered, and by 20 November the Winter War had begun. The Russians opened their offensive by bombing Finnish towns without issuing an ultimatum.

At the same time the Finnish communists in Russia set up a government at Terijoki which signed a treaty of union with the USSR. Russia could now pretend she was 'liberating' Finland, but the Finnish communist leader, Otto Kuusinen, had misled them when he encouraged them to believe that his 'government' would find supporters in Finland.

The Winter War was not at all the unopposed invasion the Red Army had expected. The Finns fought bravely for 105 days, but in February 1940, after a six-week Russian offensive in the Karelian isthmus, they were defeated, and had to sign the Treaty of Moscow in March. 11% of Finnish territory was surrendered, leaving the frontier as it had been in the days of Peter the Great. The entire population of the ceded areas retreated to the Finnish side of the new border.

This was not to be the end of the war for Finland. On 25 June, 1941 the Russians again bombed several Finnish towns, possibly misled by a statement from Hitler that Finland was entering the war on his side. Britain knew, and stated, that this was not so, but in order to placate the Russians ceased shipments of goods to Petsamo, thus throwing Finland completely into the arms of Germany. In December 1941 Britain declared war on Finland.

The 'Continuation War' went well at first, and Finland rapidly recovered territory lost in 1940, but on 9 June, 1944 there was a surprise attack by the Red Army in the Karelian isthmus and, after twelve days of fierce fighting, the Finns were driven back to north of Viipuri. This is the desperate battle so vividly described by Tikkanen towards the end of his book. The war in Finland was over.

Since the end of the Thirties there has been no language feud in Finland, perhaps because Finnish is so clearly in the ascendancy, but much work has had to be done in educational, cultural and legal spheres to accommodate two languages. It may be asked what advantages there are for Finns in having Swedish as their second language, and indeed many Finns ask it themselves, and opt for English as their second language.

Swedish culture has deep roots in Finland and is an important part of the Finnish heritage. There is no danger of its disappearance at present. Satisfactory and generous legislation protects the rights of the Swedish minority, and Swedish is still taught in schools that prepare pupils for university entrance.

The books by which Henrik Tikkanen is best known today do not fit easily into the Finnish literary scene. They are not about Finnish heroism or Finnish virtues, they are about himself. Moreover, though he has a Finnish name and is bilingual he writes his books in Swedish, for the very good reason that it is his native tongue. It also makes his books more available for translation. He had published many works which included books of travel, novels, and plays before he wrote his autobiographical trilogy *Brändövägen 8* (1976), *Bävervägen 11, Hertonäs* (1976), and *Mariegatan 26 Kronohagen* (1977), addresses at which he has lived and which have a social significance for the Finns that they lack for us. The first of these is here translated under the title of *A Winter's Day*. It was with this book that he really established his reputation as a writer.

Long before this he had made his name as a draughtsman. His drawings were often of architectural subjects, and he began to write by providing them with captions. 'These captions grew longer and longer, until at last I could publish them without pictures, and call the book a novel.' He developed his own very individual style which the critics admired, but which puzzled them because, he says: 'They did not understand that I was writing captions to pictures not included in the book.'

Mary Sandbach

About the Author

HENRIK TIKKANEN, born in Helsinki in 1924, is a
well-known Finnish novelist and artist. This is the
first volume of his three-volume autobiography.